CAULIFLOWER

RECIPES FOR SALADS, SANDWICHES, ENTRÉES AND MORE

Publications International, Ltd.

Let's get social!

@Publications_International

@PublicationsInternational

www.pilcookbooks.com

CONTENTS

INTRODUCTION

Maybe you've never thought much about cauliflower, or maybe you associate it with gloppy cheese sauce and/or bad times at the dinner table as a kid. Well, it's time to change your perspective on this pale, brain-shaped cousin of broccoli.

Actually, broccoli and cauliflower, along with brussels sprouts, cabbage and kale, are members of the Brassica family of plants; you may have noticed the relationship through the distinct cabbage-y aroma they often emit during cooking. Cauliflower originated in the northern Mediterranean region and has been enjoyed by philosophers and kings since ancient times; its name derives from Latin (caulis = cabbage + flos = flower).

This superfood's popularity has exploded recently thanks to its stellar nutritional profile (vitamin B! vitamin C! antioxidants! so much fiber!) and its ability to replace carbs like potatoes, rice and flour, making it a great option for gluten-free and low-carb diets (especially the keto and paleo diets).

This book will introduce you to the myriad ways you can incorporate cauliflower into your daily life with recipes for every level of commitment, from beginner (*Cauliflower Mac and Gouda, page 14*) to advanced (*Thai Pizza, page 92*). There's even a chapter of broccoli recipes because 1) they're a natural pair and 2) broccoli is delicious. Keep reading for some basics on the four main ways to prepare cauliflower, or explore the recipes and then come back to learn more.

RAW/MARINATED: Chopped raw cauliflower makes a nice addition to salads or can even BE the salad (see *Broccoli and Cauliflower Salad, page 136*). All you have to do is chop it up and throw it in and you're done. It's also a natural as part of a crudité selection, and is excellent dipped in hummus, spinach dip and ranch dressing. Cauliflower readily takes on the flavor of marinades and retains a pleasant crunch

even after a long soak. Try the *Cauliflower Caprese Salad on page 132* or *Spicy Pickled Relish on page 134* to see for yourself. Stick to smaller pieces (think bite-size or smaller) for marinating so that the marinade can thoroughly infuse the cauliflower, and then you don't have to cut it up after marinating.

STEAMED/BOILED/MASHED: When steaming cauliflower, doneness is a matter of personal taste. In some of the recipes in this book, it matters that the cauliflower retains some bite (*Cauliflower Picnic Salad, page 108*) or that it is cooked until very tender (*Cauliflower Mash, page 130*), but for your own purposes, cook it to any degree of doneness. To boil cauliflower, fill a large saucepan of water with a few inches of water and add 1 teaspoon of salt. Bring the water to a boil over high heat. Add the cauliflower, reduce the heat to medium-low, cover it and cook 10 to 20 minutes until it's the desired degree of tenderness. You can also steam it in a steamer basket in a saucepan or in the microwave. To microwave, place the cauliflower florets in a large microwavable bowl, add 2 tablespoons water, cover and cook 5 minutes on HIGH or until tender.

CAULIFLOWER RICE: Riced cauliflower (cauliflower chopped up into tiny rice-size pieces) makes a great low-carb substitute for regular rice and couscous in many recipes. Frozen cauliflower rice is readily available in large grocery stores, but it is also quite easy to make at home.

Method 1: Use a food processor

Your food processor makes quick work of cauliflower. Cut the head of cauliflower into 1-inch florets. Working in batches, pulse the florets until they form small rice-size pieces. If there are any large chunks left behind, pick them out and add them to your next batch.

Method 2: Use a box grater

A box grater produces similar results to the food processor. Leave the cauliflower head whole. Working over a large bowl, grate the head of cauliflower on the large holes of the grater, rotating until all the florets are gone.

Method 3: Use a knife

If you'd like chunkier cauliflower, use a chef's knife to coarsely chop the head of cauliflower into small pieces. This works well for recipes where the cauliflower may disappear when it's mixed into other ingredients like in the *Mexican Cauliflower and Bean Skillet, page 66* and the *Quinoa and Cauliflower Taco Salad, page 138.*

To cook riced cauliflower to serve alongside other ingredients (as in the *Turkey Taco Bowls, page 58*), place it in a large microwavable bowl, season it with salt, if desired, and cover with plastic wrap. Cut a small slit in the plastic wrap to vent and then microwave on HIGH 4 minutes. Stir, cover it again and microwave for an additional 4 minutes. If you're using frozen cauliflower rice, heat it according to the package directions or use as the recipe directs.

ROASTED CAULIFLOWER: Roasting cauliflower is the best way to bring out its nutty flavor. As with steaming, you can roast cauliflower for a shorter time (25 minutes) or a longer time (45 minutes to an hour) depending on how you like it. Most recipes in this book call for a roasting time of about 30 to 35 minutes, but feel free to roast as much or as little as you like. See the recipe at right for directions on making perfect roasted cauliflower that you can enjoy plain or add to any pasta, grain or salad recipe.

ROASTED CAULIFLOWER
MAKES 4 SERVINGS

1 head cauliflower, cut into 1-inch florets

2 tablespoons olive oil

1½ teaspoons spices or seasonings (optional; see note)

Salt and black pepper

1 Preheat oven to 425°F. Spray sheet pan with nonstick cooking spray.

2 Place cauliflower on prepared sheet pan. Drizzle with oil. Sprinkle evenly with seasoning, if desired, and season with salt and pepper. Toss to coat; arrange in single layer.

3 Roast 25 to 45 minutes or until tender and browned, stirring once or twice.

NOTE

For seasonings, use curry powder, garam masala or Italian seasoning with a bit of minced fresh garlic. Or try a mix of chili powder, chipotle chili powder, cumin and oregano.

PASTA

**LEMON CREAM PASTA
WITH ROASTED CAULIFLOWER
8**

**CAULIFLOWER
MAC AND GOUDA
14**

**WHOLE WHEAT SPAGHETTI
WITH CAULIFLOWER AND FETA
16**

**CREAMY HERB
MAC AND CHEESE**
10

PASTA PRIMAVERA
12

QUICK AND EASY PASTA SALAD
18

SOBA TERIYAKI BOWL
20

LEMON CREAM PASTA WITH ROASTED CAULIFLOWER

MAKES 6 TO 8 SERVINGS

1 head cauliflower, cut into 1-inch florets

2 tablespoons olive oil

1 teaspoon salt, divided

¼ teaspoon plus ⅛ teaspoon black pepper, divided

8 ounces uncooked cavatappi or rotini pasta

¼ cup (½ stick) butter, cut into pieces

¼ cup all-purpose flour

2 cups milk

½ cup shredded Parmesan cheese

Grated peel and juice of 1 lemon

¼ cup chopped almonds, toasted*

Baby arugula

Crushed Aleppo pepper or red pepper flakes (optional)

To toast almonds, spread in single layer in heavy skillet. Cook over medium heat 1 to 2 minutes or until nuts are lightly browned, stirring frequently.

1 Preheat oven to 425°F. Place cauliflower on sheet pan. Drizzle with oil and sprinkle with ½ teaspoon salt and ¼ teaspoon black pepper; toss to coat. Roast 30 to 35 minutes or until cauliflower is well browned and tender, stirring once.

2 Cook pasta in large saucepan of boiling salted water according to package directions until al dente. Drain, reserving 1 cup pasta cooking water. Place pasta in large bowl; add cauliflower.

3 Melt butter in same saucepan over medium heat; whisk in flour until smooth paste forms. Gradually whisk in milk, remaining ½ teaspoon salt and ⅛ teaspoon black pepper; cook 2 to 3 minutes or until thickened. Whisk in ½ cup reserved pasta water and Parmesan until smooth. Pour over pasta and cauliflower; stir to coat. Add additional pasta water by tablespoonfuls to loosen sauce, if needed. Stir in lemon peel and juice and almonds. Top with arugula or gently fold into pasta. Sprinkle with Aleppo pepper.

NOTE

Aleppo pepper is a kind of chile similar to red pepper flakes (crushed red pepper) but milder and sweeter in flavor. It is a common ingredient in Middle Eastern and Mediterranean cooking, but in can be hard to find. It is work seeking out online or in specialty stores as it complements many different types of dishes.

CREAMY HERB MAC AND CHEESE

MAKES 4 TO 6 SERVINGS

3 cups uncooked whole wheat macaroni

3 cups finely chopped cauliflower florets*

2 tablespoons butter

2 tablespoons all-purpose flour

2 tablespoons minced onion

3 cloves garlic, minced

½ teaspoon salt, divided

1¼ cups milk

¼ cup half-and-half

1 teaspoon chopped fresh thyme

3 garlic-and-herb spreadable cheese wedges (about 1 ounce each)

2 tablespoons grated Parmesan cheese

See page 5 (method 3).

1 Cook pasta in large saucepan of boiling salted water according to package directions until al dente. Add cauliflower during last 5 minutes of cooking time. Drain pasta and cauliflower.

2 Melt butter in medium skillet over medium heat; whisk in flour until smooth paste forms. Add onion, garlic and ¼ teaspoon salt; cook and stir 1 minute or until onion is softened. Gradually whisk in milk and half-and-half until well blended. Cook 2 to 3 minutes or until sauce boils and is thickened, whisking constantly. Whisk in thyme and remaining ¼ teaspoon salt.

3 Remove from heat. Whisk in cheese wedges until cheese is melted and sauce is smooth. Stir in pasta and cauliflower until combined. Stir in Parmesan.

PASTA PRIMAVERA
MAKES 4 SERVINGS

1 package (16 ounces)
   uncooked linguine

1 cup broccoli florets

1 cup bite-size
   cauliflower florets

1 carrot, thinly sliced

3 tablespoons olive oil

   Salt and black pepper

1 red bell pepper, thinly
   sliced

1 yellow bell pepper,
   thinly sliced

½ cup snow peas

½ cup sliced shiitake,
   morel or chanterelle
   mushrooms

2 cloves garlic, minced

4 fresh basil leaves,
   minced

   Grated Parmesan
   cheese (optional)

1 Cook pasta in large saucepan of boiling salted water according to package directions until al dente. Drain and place in large bowl; keep warm.

2 Meanwhile, steam broccoli, cauliflower and carrot in steamer basket in saucepan or in large microwavable bowl 3 minutes or until crisp-tender.

3 Heat oil in large skillet over medium heat. Add steamed vegetables, bell peppers, snow peas, mushrooms and garlic; cook and stir 3 to 5 minutes or until bell peppers are crisp-tender. Season with salt and black pepper. Add to pasta; toss to coat. Sprinkle with basil; serve immediately with Parmesan, if desired.

CAULIFLOWER MAC AND GOUDA

MAKES 6 TO 8 SERVINGS

1 package (16 ounces) uncooked bowtie pasta

1 head cauliflower, cut into 1-inch florets

4 cups milk

2 cloves garlic, peeled and smashed

¼ cup (½ stick) plus 3 tablespoons butter, divided

5 tablespoons all-purpose flour

1 teaspoon dry mustard

⅛ teaspoon smoked or regular paprika

1 pound Gouda cheese, shredded

Salt and black pepper

1 cup panko bread crumbs

1 Cook pasta in large saucepan of boiling salted water according to package directions until al dente. Scoop out pasta with large slotted spoon; place in large bowl and keep warm. Return water to a boil. Add cauliflower; cook 3 to 5 minutes or just until tender. Drain and add to pasta.

2 Meanwhile, bring milk and garlic to a boil in small saucepan. Remove from heat. Discard garlic.

3 Melt ¼ cup butter in large saucepan over medium heat; whisk in flour until smooth paste forms. Stir in mustard and paprika. Gradually whisk in warm milk; bring to a boil. Reduce heat to medium-low; cook 5 to 7 minutes or until thickened, whisking frequently. Gradually whisk in cheese until melted. Season with salt and pepper. Add pasta and cauliflower; mix well.

4 Preheat broiler. Spread pasta mixture in 13×9-inch baking dish.

5 Melt remaining 3 tablespoons butter in small saucepan over medium heat. Add panko; stir just until moistened. Sprinkle panko mixture over pasta mixture. Broil 2 minutes or until golden brown.

WHOLE WHEAT SPAGHETTI WITH CAULIFLOWER AND FETA

MAKES 4 SERVINGS

3 tablespoons olive oil

1 onion, chopped

4 cloves garlic, minced

1 head cauliflower, cut into 1-inch florets

⅔ cup white wine or vegetable broth

1 teaspoon salt

½ teaspoon black pepper

8 ounces uncooked whole wheat spaghetti

1 pint grape tomatoes, cut in half

½ cup coarsely chopped walnuts

¼ teaspoon red pepper flakes (optional)

½ cup crumbled feta cheese

1 Heat oil in large skillet over medium heat. Add onion; cook and stir 5 minutes or until softened. Add garlic; cook and stir 1 minute. Add cauliflower; cook and stir 5 minutes. Add wine, salt and pepper. Cover and cook about 15 minutes or until cauliflower is crisp-tender.

2 Meanwhile, cook pasta in large saucepan of boiling salted water according to package directions until al dente. Reserve ½ cup pasta cooking water; drain pasta and keep warm.

3 Add tomatoes, walnuts and reserved pasta water to skillet; season with red pepper flakes, if desired. Cook 2 to 3 minutes or until tomatoes begin to soften.

4 Toss spaghetti with cauliflower mixture in skillet or serving bowl; top with feta.

QUICK AND EASY PASTA SALAD

MAKES 4 TO 6 SERVINGS

8 ounces uncooked campanelle, cellentani or rotini pasta

1½ cups bite-size cauliflower florets

1½ cups sliced carrots

1½ cups snow peas

½ cup Italian salad dressing or balsamic vinaigrette

4 ounces crumbled feta cheese, blue cheese, shredded Parmesan cheese or fresh mozzarella pearls (optional)

1 Cook pasta in large saucepan of boiling salted water according to package directions until al dente, adding cauliflower, carrots and snow peas during last 3 minutes of cooking time. Drain pasta and vegetables. Run under cold water to stop cooking; drain well. Transfer to large bowl.

2 Add salad dressing to pasta and vegetable mixture; stir to coat. Stir in cheese, if desired. Refrigerate until ready to serve.

NOTE

This pasta salad can be made ahead of time. Just before serving, stir in a few additional tablespoonfuls of dressing to refresh the salad.

SOBA TERIYAKI BOWL
MAKES 4 SERVINGS

¾ cup plus 1 tablespoon cornstarch, divided

2 teaspoons salt, divided

½ cup plus 2 tablespoons water, divided

1 head cauliflower, cut into 1-inch florets

¾ cup pineapple juice

¾ cup soy sauce

2 tablespoons packed brown sugar

1 tablespoon lime juice

1 teaspoon minced garlic

6 ounces uncooked soba noodles

5 cups shredded red, green or mixed cabbage or 1 package (14 ounces) coleslaw mix

½ cup unseasoned rice vinegar

1 teaspoon granulated sugar

2 green onions, chopped

1 tablespoon sesame seeds

1 Preheat oven to 400°F. Spray sheet pan with nonstick cooking spray. Whisk ¾ cup cornstarch and 1 teaspoon salt in medium bowl. Whisk in ½ cup water until smooth. Dip cauliflower into mixture; place in single layer on prepared sheet pan. Bake 20 minutes or until tender.

2 Meanwhile, bring pineapple juice, soy sauce, brown sugar, lime juice and garlic to a simmer in small saucepan. Whisk 2 tablespoons water into 1 tablespoon cornstarch in small bowl; stir into sauce. Reduce heat to low; cook and stir 5 minutes. Transfer to large bowl; cool slightly. Remove ¼ cup sauce; set aside.

3 Cook soba noodles according to package directions. Drain and rinse under cold water until cool. Divide among serving bowls.

4 Combine cabbage, vinegar, granulated sugar and remaining 1 teaspoon salt in medium bowl; mix and squeeze with hands until well blended.

5 Add cauliflower to large bowl of sauce; stir to coat. Divide among serving bowls. Drizzle some of reserved sauce over noodles. Serve with cabbage mixture. Sprinkle with green onions and sesame seeds.

STIR-FRIES & CURRIES

**TOFU CAULIFLOWER
FRIED RICE
24**

**EASY ORANGE CHICKEN
36**

**CURRIED CAULIFLOWER
RICE AND VERMICELLI
38**

**THAI VEGGIE CURRY
40**

**CURRIED CAULIFLOWER
AND POTATOES
42**

**PORK CURRY OVER
CAULIFLOWER COUSCOUS
34**

PUMPKIN CURRY
28

CAULIFLOWER AND
POTATO MASALA
30

BIBIMBAP WITH
CAULIFLOWER RICE
32

LENTIL RICE CURRY
26

CHICKEN AND VEGETABLE
CURRY NOODLE BOWL
44

CURRIED CAULIFLOWER
AND CASHEWS
46

TOFU CAULIFLOWER FRIED RICE

MAKES 4 SERVINGS

3 tablespoons soy sauce

1 tablespoon plus 1 teaspoon minced fresh ginger, divided

2 teaspoons dark sesame oil

1 teaspoon packed brown sugar

1 teaspoon rice vinegar

1 package (14 ounces) firm tofu, drained and cut into 1-inch cubes

2 tablespoons vegetable oil, divided

1 medium yellow onion, chopped

1 carrot, chopped

½ cup frozen peas

2 cloves garlic, minced

1 package (about 12 ounces) frozen cauliflower rice

1 green onion, thinly sliced

1 Whisk soy sauce, 1 tablespoon ginger, sesame oil, brown sugar and vinegar in small bowl. Place tofu in quart-size resealable food storage bag. Pour marinade over tofu. Seal bag, pressing out as much air as possible. Turn to coat tofu with marinade. Refrigerate 3 hours or overnight.

2 Drain tofu, reserving marinade. Heat 1 tablespoon vegetable oil in large skillet over high heat. Add tofu; stir-fry 3 to 5 minutes or until edges are browned. Transfer to bowl.

3 Heat remaining 1 tablespoon vegetable oil in same skillet. Add yellow onion and carrot; stir-fry 2 minutes or until softened. Add peas, garlic and remaining 1 teaspoon ginger; cook 2 minutes or until peas are hot. Add frozen cauliflower rice and ¼ cup reserved marinade; stir-fry 5 minutes or until heated through. Return tofu to skillet; stir-fry until heated through. Top with green onion.

LENTIL RICE CURRY
MAKES 6 SERVINGS

2 tablespoons olive oil

1 cup sliced green onions

3 cloves garlic, minced

2 tablespoons minced fresh ginger

2 teaspoons curry powder

½ teaspoon ground cumin

½ teaspoon ground turmeric

3 cups water

1 can (about 14 ounces) diced tomatoes

½ teaspoon salt

1 cup dried red lentils, rinsed and sorted

1 head cauliflower, cut into 1-inch florets

1 tablespoon lemon juice

Fragrant Basmati Rice (recipe follows) *or* 4 cups hot cooked jasmine rice

1 Heat oil in large saucepan over medium heat. Add green onions, garlic, ginger, curry powder, cumin and turmeric; cook and stir 5 minutes. Add water, tomatoes and salt; bring to a boil over high heat.

2 Stir in lentils. Reduce heat to low; cover and simmer 35 to 40 minutes or until lentils are tender. Add cauliflower and lemon juice. Cover and simmer 8 to 10 minutes more or until cauliflower is tender.

3 Meanwhile, prepare Fragrant Basmati Rice, if desired. Serve with lentil curry.

FRAGRANT BASMATI RICE

Bring 2 cups apple juice, ¾ cup water and ½ teaspoon salt to a boil in medium saucepan. Add 1½ cups uncooked basmati rice, 2 thin slices of fresh ginger and 1 cinnamon stick. Reduce heat to low; cover and simmer 25 to 30 minutes or until liquid is absorbed. Remove and discard ginger and cinnamon stick. Makes 4 cups.

PUMPKIN CURRY
MAKES 4 SERVINGS

1 tablespoon vegetable oil

1 package (14 ounces) firm tofu, drained, patted dry and cut into 1-inch cubes

¼ cup Thai red curry paste

2 cloves garlic, minced

1 can (15 ounces) pumpkin purée

1 can (13 ounces) coconut milk

1 cup vegetable broth

1½ teaspoons salt

1 teaspoon sriracha sauce

1 cup broccoli florets

1 cup bite-size cauliflower florets

1 cup cubed peeled sweet potato

1 red bell pepper, cubed

½ cup peas

Hot cooked rice

¼ cup shredded fresh basil (optional)

1 Heat oil in wok or large skillet over high heat. Add tofu; stir-fry 5 minutes or until lightly browned. Add curry paste and garlic; cook and stir 1 minute or until tofu is coated.

2 Add pumpkin, coconut milk, broth, salt and sriracha; bring to a boil. Stir in broccoli, cauliflower, sweet potato and bell pepper. Reduce heat to medium; cover and simmer 20 minutes or until vegetables are tender.

3 Stir in peas; cook 1 minute or until heated through. Serve over rice; top with basil, if desired.

CAULIFLOWER AND POTATO MASALA

MAKES 6 SERVINGS

2 tablespoons vegetable oil

1 teaspoon minced garlic

1 teaspoon finely chopped fresh ginger

1 teaspoon salt

1 teaspoon cumin seeds

1 teaspoon ground coriander

1½ cups chopped tomatoes, fresh or canned

1 head cauliflower, cut into 1-inch florets

8 ounces medium red potatoes, peeled and cut into wedges

½ teaspoon garam masala

2 tablespoons chopped fresh cilantro

1 Heat oil in large saucepan over medium-high heat. Add garlic, ginger, salt, cumin and coriander; cook and stir 30 seconds or until fragrant.

2 Add tomatoes; cook and stir 1 minute. Add cauliflower and potatoes; mix well. Reduce heat to low; cover and cook about 30 minutes or until vegetables are tender.

3 Stir in garam masala; mix well. Pour into serving bowl; sprinkle with cilantro.

BIBIMBAP WITH CAULIFLOWER RICE

MAKES 4 TO 6 SERVINGS

3 tablespoons soy sauce, divided

1 tablespoon packed brown sugar

1½ teaspoons dark sesame oil

3 cloves garlic, minced, divided

12 ounces beef for stir-fry

1 seedless cucumber, thinly sliced

⅓ cup rice vinegar

¼ teaspoon plus ⅛ teaspoon salt, divided

2 tablespoons plus 1 teaspoon vegetable oil, divided

4 ounces shiitake mushrooms, stemmed and sliced

3 cups fresh spinach

1 tablespoon water

3 cups frozen cauliflower rice, cooked according to package directions

1 carrot, julienned

4 eggs, cooked sunny side up or over easy

Gochujang sauce or sriracha sauce

1 Combine 2 tablespoons soy sauce, brown sugar, sesame oil and 1 clove garlic in medium bowl. Add beef; stir to thoroughly coat with marinade. Refrigerate 30 minutes to 1 hour.

2 For marinated cucumbers, combine cucumbers, vinegar and ⅛ teaspoon salt in large bowl. Let stand at room temperature until ready to serve.

3 For mushrooms, heat 1 tablespoon vegetable oil in medium skillet over high heat. Add mushrooms and remaining ¼ teaspoon salt; cook and stir 2 to 3 minutes or until mushrooms are browned and tender. Transfer to medium bowl.

4 For spinach, heat 1 teaspoon vegetable oil in same skillet over high heat. Add spinach and 1 tablespoon water; cook until spinach is wilted. Add remaining 2 cloves garlic; cook 30 seconds or until garlic is lightly browned. Stir in remaining 1 tablespoon soy sauce. Transfer spinach to another medium bowl.

5 For beef, heat remaining 1 tablespoon vegetable oil in same skillet over high heat. Add beef and marinade; cook and stir 2 to 3 minutes or until beef is no longer pink.

6 For each serving, divide cauliflower rice among serving bowls. Top with cucumbers, carrots, spinach, mushrooms and beef. Top with egg, if desired, and serve with desired sauce.

PORK CURRY OVER CAULIFLOWER COUSCOUS

MAKES 6 SERVINGS

3 tablespoons olive oil, divided

2 tablespoons mild curry powder

2 teaspoons minced garlic

1½ pounds boneless pork (shoulder, loin or chops), cubed

1 red or green bell pepper, diced

1 tablespoon cider vinegar

½ teaspoon salt

2 cups water

1 head cauliflower, riced (see page 4)

1 Heat 2 tablespoons oil in large saucepan over medium heat. Add curry powder and garlic; cook and stir 1 to 2 minutes or until garlic is golden.

2 Add pork; cook and stir 5 to 7 minutes or until pork cubes are barely pink in center. Add bell pepper and vinegar; cook and stir 3 minutes or until bell pepper is soft. Sprinkle with salt.

3 Add water; bring to a boil. Reduce heat and simmer 30 to 45 minutes, stirring occasionally, until liquid is reduced and pork is tender, adding additional water as needed.

4 Heat remaining 1 tablespoon oil in 12-inch nonstick skillet over medium heat. Add cauliflower; cook and stir 5 minutes or until crisp-tender. *Do not overcook.* Serve pork curry over cauliflower.

EASY ORANGE CHICKEN

MAKES 4 SERVINGS

3 tablespoons frozen orange juice concentrate, thawed

2 tablespoons water

2 tablespoons soy sauce

¾ teaspoon cornstarch

¼ teaspoon garlic powder

3 teaspoons canola oil, divided

2 carrots, sliced

1 cup bite-size cauliflower florets

1 cup broccoli florets

12 ounces boneless skinless chicken breasts, cut into bite-size pieces

3 cups hot cooked rice

1 Combine orange juice concentrate, water, soy sauce, cornstarch and garlic powder in small bowl; stir until smooth.

2 Heat 1 teaspoon oil in wok or large nonstick skillet. Add carrots; stir-fry over high heat 1 minute. Add cauliflower and broccoli; stir-fry 2 to 3 minutes or until vegetables are crisp-tender. Transfer vegetables to medium bowl.

3 Add remaining 2 teaspoons oil to wok; heat over medium-high heat. Add chicken; stir-fry 2 to 3 minutes or until cooked through. Push chicken up side of wok. Stir sauce mixture; add to wok. Bring to a boil. Return vegetables to wok; cook and stir until heated through. Serve over rice.

TIP

To cut carrots decoratively, use a citrus stripper or grapefruit spoon to cut 4 or 5 grooves into whole carrots, cutting lengthwise from stem end to tip. Then cut carrots crosswise into slices.

CURRIED CAULIFLOWER WITH RICE AND VERMICELLI

MAKES 2 TO 4 SERVINGS

2	teaspoons canola or vegetable oil
1	cup finely chopped onion
1	clove garlic, minced
1	teaspoon curry powder
½	teaspoon ground coriander
¼	teaspoon salt
½	cup uncooked long grain rice
½	cup broken vermicelli (1-inch pieces)
1	cup apple juice
½	cup water
3	cups bite-size cauliflower florets
3	tablespoons golden raisins

1 Heat oil in large nonstick skillet over medium heat. Add onion and garlic; cook and stir 2 minutes. Add curry powder, coriander and salt; cook and stir 1 minute. Stir in rice and vermicelli until coated with spices. Remove skillet from heat.

2 Bring apple juice and water to a boil in small saucepan; pour over rice and vermicelli mixture. Bring mixture to a boil over high heat. Reduce heat to low. Cover and simmer 15 minutes.

3 Set cauliflower and raisins on top of rice mixture. Cover and simmer about 7 minutes or until water is absorbed. Stir cauliflower and raisins into mixture. Remove from heat; let stand, covered, 5 minutes or until cauliflower is crisp-tender. Fluff with fork before serving.

THAI VEGGIE CURRY

MAKES 4 TO 6 SERVINGS

2 tablespoons vegetable oil

1 onion, quartered and thinly sliced

1 tablespoon Thai red curry paste (or to taste)

1 can (about 13 ounces) unsweetened coconut milk

2 red or yellow bell peppers, cut into strips

2 cups bite-size cauliflower florets

½ cup broccoli florets

1 cup snow peas

1 package (14 ounces) tofu, pressed and cubed

Salt and black pepper

¼ cup slivered fresh basil

Hot cooked jasmine rice

1 Heat oil in large skillet or wok over medium-high heat. Add onion; cook and stir 2 minutes or until softened. Add curry paste; cook and stir to coat onion. Add coconut milk; bring to a boil, stirring to dissolve curry paste.

2 Add bell peppers, cauliflower and broccoli; simmer over medium heat 4 to 5 minutes or until crisp-tender. Stir in snow peas; simmer 2 minutes. Gently stir in tofu; cook until heated through. Season with salt and pepper.

3 Sprinkle with basil; serve with rice.

CURRIED CAULIFLOWER AND POTATOES

MAKES 6 SERVINGS

3 tablespoons vegetable oil

1 medium onion, chopped

1 tablespoon minced garlic

1 tablespoon curry powder

1½ teaspoons salt

1½ teaspoons grated fresh ginger

1 teaspoon ground turmeric

1 teaspoon yellow or brown mustard seeds

¼ teaspoon red pepper flakes

½ cup water

1 head cauliflower, cut into 1-inch florets

1½ pounds fingerling potatoes, cut into halves

1 Heat oil in large saucepan over medium-high heat. Add onion; cook and stir about 5 minutes or until beginning to brown. Add garlic, curry powder, salt, ginger, turmeric, mustard seeds and red pepper flakes; cook and stir 1 minute. Stir in water, scraping up browned bits from bottom of saucepan. Stir in cauliflower and potatoes; mix well.

2 Reduce heat to medium-low; cover and cook 15 minutes or until potatoes and cauliflower are tender.

CHICKEN AND VEGETABLE CURRY NOODLE BOWL

MAKES 4 SERVINGS

8 ounces uncooked whole wheat egg noodles

12 ounces boneless skinless chicken breasts or chicken tenders, cut into bite-size pieces

2 tablespoons all-purpose flour

2 teaspoons curry powder

½ teaspoon salt

¼ teaspoon red pepper flakes (optional)

1 tablespoon canola oil

1 cup chicken broth

2 cups bite-size cauliflower florets

1 cup broccoli florets

1 red bell pepper, diced

2 tablespoons sliced almonds

1 Cook pasta in large saucepan of boiling salted water according to package directions until al dente. Drain and return to saucepan; keep warm.

2 Combine chicken, flour, curry powder, salt and red pepper flakes, if desired, in medium bowl; toss to coat.

3 Heat oil in large deep skillet or wok over medium heat. Add chicken mixture; stir-fry 3 to 4 minutes or until chicken is no longer pink on outside.

4 Add broth and vegetables; bring to a boil. Simmer about 8 minutes or until chicken is cooked through and sauce is slightly thickened. Serve over noodles; sprinkle with almonds.

CURRIED CAULIFLOWER AND CASHEWS
MAKES 8 SERVINGS

1 head cauliflower, cut into 1-inch florets (about 4 cups)

½ cup water

1 cup toasted cashews, divided

3 tablespoons butter, divided

2 tablespoons all-purpose flour

1 tablespoon curry powder

1¼ cups milk

Salt and black pepper

1 cup plain dry bread crumbs or panko bread crumbs

Prepared mango chutney (optional)

1 Preheat oven to 350°F. Spray 2-quart baking dish with nonstick cooking spray.

2 Place cauliflower in large microwavable bowl. Add water; cover and microwave on HIGH about 4 minutes or until almost tender. Drain and place in prepared baking dish. Stir in ¾ cup cashews.

3 Melt 2 tablespoons butter in medium saucepan over medium heat. Whisk in flour and curry powder until smooth paste forms; cook and stir 2 minutes. Gradually whisk in milk; cook and stir until mixture thickens slightly, whisking constantly. Season with salt and pepper.

4 Pour sauce over cauliflower mixture; stir to coat. Top with bread crumbs. Dot with remaining 1 tablespoon butter.

5 Bake 45 minutes or until lightly browned. Garnish with remaining ¼ cup cashews; serve with chutney, if desired.

ENTRÉES

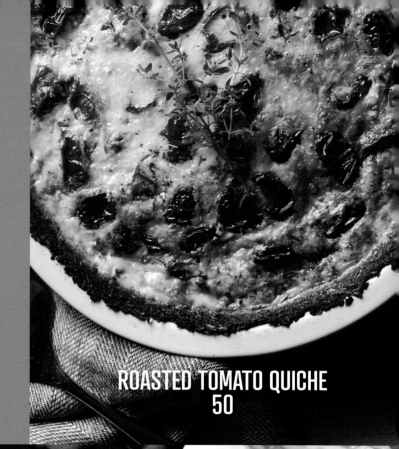

ROASTED TOMATO QUICHE
50

BISCUIT-TOPPED CHICKEN POT PIE
56

TURKEY TACO BOWLS
58

**BACON AND EGG
BREAKFAST CASSEROLE
52**

**CAULIFLOWER PARMESAN
54**

**WHOLE ROASTED
CAULIFLOWER
60**

**CORNMEAL-CRUSTED
CAULIFLOWER STEAKS
62**

**CAULIFLOWER, SAUSAGE
AND GOUDA SHEET PAN
64**

**MEXICAN CAULIFLOWER
AND BEAN SKILLET
66**

ROASTED TOMATO QUICHE

MAKES 6 TO 8 SERVINGS

1 pint grape tomatoes

1 tablespoon olive oil

Salt and black pepper

2½ cups riced cauliflower (fresh or frozen; see page 4)

½ cup shredded Parmesan cheese

6 eggs, divided

¾ cup milk

½ cup (2 ounces) shredded mozzarella cheese

2 cloves garlic, minced

½ teaspoon fresh thyme leaves

1 Preheat oven to 350°F. Place tomatoes in shallow baking dish; drizzle with oil and sprinkle lightly with salt and pepper. Bake 1 hour, stirring once or twice.

2 Spray 9-inch pie plate with nonstick cooking spray. Place cauliflower in large microwavable bowl; cover with plastic wrap and cut slit to vent. Microwave on HIGH 4 minutes; stir. Cover and cook on HIGH 4 minutes. Remove cover; cool slightly. Place cauliflower on double layer of paper towels; fold over paper towels and squeeze to remove excess moisture. Return to bowl. Add Parmesan, 1 egg, ½ teaspoon salt and ¼ teaspoon pepper; mix well. Press onto bottom and up side of prepared pie plate. *Increase oven temperature to 425°F.* Bake crust 15 minutes. Remove from oven; place on sheet pan.

3 *Reduce oven temperature to 375°F.* Whisk remaining 5 eggs, milk, mozzarella, garlic, thyme, ¼ teaspoon salt and a dash of black pepper in medium bowl until well blended. Place tomatoes in crust; pour egg mixture over tomatoes. Bake 45 minutes or until thin knife inserted into center comes out clean (a little cheese is okay). Cool 10 minutes before slicing.

BACON AND EGG BREAKFAST CASSEROLE
MAKES 6 SERVINGS

CRUST

- 2 cups riced cauliflower (fresh or frozen; see page 4)
- ½ cup shredded Parmesan cheese
- 1 egg
- ½ teaspoon salt
- ⅛ teaspoon ground red pepper (optional)

FILLING

- 1 package (about 12 ounces) bacon, chopped
- 1 onion, chopped
- 1 jalapeño pepper, seeded and chopped
- 2 cloves garlic, minced
- 1 cup (4 ounces) shredded Cheddar cheese, divided
- 8 eggs
- ¾ cup milk
- ¼ teaspoon salt

1 Preheat oven to 400°F. For crust, place cauliflower in 8-inch glass baking dish; cover with plastic wrap and cut slit to vent. Microwave on HIGH 6 minutes. Remove cover; cool slightly. Firmly blot and squeeze cauliflower with paper towels to remove excess moisture. Add Parmesan, 1 egg, ½ teaspoon salt and red pepper, if desired; mix well. Press onto bottom and up side of baking dish. Bake 15 minutes. Remove from oven. *Reduce oven temperature to 350°F.*

2 Meanwhile for filling, cook bacon in large skillet over medium heat until crisp. Remove with slotted spoon to paper towels to drain. Drain all but 1 tablespoon drippings from skillet; return to medium heat. Add onion; cook and stir 5 minutes or until onion is softened. Add jalapeño and garlic; cook and stir 30 seconds. Remove from heat. Place onion mixture and all but ¼ cup bacon in crust; sprinkle with ¾ cup Cheddar cheese.

3 Whisk 8 eggs, milk and ¼ teaspoon salt in large bowl until well blended. Pour into crust.

4 Bake 30 minutes. Sprinkle with remaining ¼ cup Cheddar cheese and remaining bacon; bake 5 minutes or until cheese is melted and thin knife inserted into center comes out clean.

CAULIFLOWER PARMESAN
MAKES 4 SERVINGS

2 heads cauliflower (about 2 pounds each)

1 tablespoon plus 2 teaspoons olive oil, divided

2 teaspoons salt, divided

Black pepper

3 tablespoons butter

1 medium sweet onion, chopped

2 cloves garlic, minced

1 teaspoon dried oregano

½ teaspoon dried basil

¼ teaspoon red pepper flakes (optional)

1 can (28 ounces) crushed tomatoes

1 can (about 14 ounces) diced tomatoes

⅓ cup shredded Parmesan cheese

4 slices fresh mozzarella cheese (1 ounce each)

Shredded fresh basil

1 Preheat oven to 425°F. Turn cauliflower stem side up on cutting board. Trim away leaves, leaving stem intact. Slice through stem into 2 or 3 slices. Trim off excess florets from two end slices, creating flat "steaks." Repeat with remaining cauliflower; reserve extra cauliflower for another use.

2 Grease large baking sheet with 2 teaspoons oil. Place 4 steaks on baking sheet. Brush remaining 1 tablespoon oil over cauliflower; sprinkle with 1 teaspoon salt and season with pepper. Bake 25 minutes or until fork-tender and well browned.

3 Meanwhile for sauce, melt butter in large saucepan over medium-high heat. Add onion; cook and stir 5 minutes or until softened. Add garlic, remaining 1 teaspoon salt, oregano, basil and red pepper flakes, if desired; cook and stir 1 minute. Add tomatoes; mix well. Bring to a simmer. Reduce heat to medium; partially cover and cook 20 minutes.

4 *Reduce oven temperature to 375°F.* Spray 13×9-inch baking pan with nonstick cooking spray. Spread 2 cups sauce in pan. Using large spatula, carefully transfer cauliflower to baking pan. Spread ¼ cup sauce over each steak; sprinkle evenly with Parmesan. Top with slice of mozzarella.

5 Bake 12 to 15 minutes or until sauce is bubbly and cheese is melted. Serve with remaining sauce or reserve for another use. Sprinkle with basil.

BISCUIT-TOPPED CHICKEN POT PIE

MAKES 6 SERVINGS

1½ pounds boneless skinless chicken breasts, cut into 1-inch pieces

¼ cup chicken broth

2 cups bite-size cauliflower florets

1 cup broccoli florets

1 small zucchini, quartered lengthwise and thinly sliced

1 red bell pepper, chopped

1 carrot, sliced

1 can (10¾ ounces) condensed cream of chicken soup, undiluted

4 tablespoons grated Parmesan cheese, divided

1 teaspoon dried thyme

½ teaspoon black pepper

1½ cups biscuit baking mix

½ cup milk

1 Preheat oven to 400°F.

2 Combine chicken and broth in large saucepan; bring to a boil over high heat. Reduce heat; simmer 8 minutes or until chicken is cooked through, stirring occasionally. Stir in cauliflower, broccoli, zucchini, bell pepper, carrot, soup, 2 tablespoons cheese, thyme and pepper; mix well. Cook until heated through. Transfer mixture to 8-inch square baking dish.

3 Combine baking mix and milk in small bowl; mix just until moistened. Drop batter by heaping tablespoonfuls over hot chicken mixture; sprinkle with remaining 2 tablespoons cheese.

4 Bake 14 to 16 minutes or until bubbly and biscuits are golden brown.

TURKEY TACO BOWLS
MAKES 4 SERVINGS

1 pound ground turkey

1 package (1 ounce) taco seasoning mix

¾ cup water

1 package (about 12 ounces) frozen cauliflower rice

2 cups shredded red cabbage

2 green onions, finely chopped

1 avocado, thinly sliced

2 plum tomatoes, diced

Minced fresh cilantro, sour cream and crumbled cotija cheese

1 Cook turkey in large nonstick skillet over medium-high heat 6 to 8 minutes or until no longer pink, stirring to break up meat. Stir in taco seasoning mix and water; bring to a boil. Reduce heat to medium-low; simmer 5 minutes, stirring occasionally.

2 Heat cauliflower rice according to package directions. Divide among four bowls. Add turkey, cabbage, green onions, avocado and tomatoes. Serve with cilantro, sour cream and cotija cheese.

ENTRÉES

WHOLE ROASTED CAULIFLOWER
MAKES 4 TO 6 SERVINGS

6 tablespoons olive oil, divided

1 head cauliflower, leaves trimmed

½ teaspoon plus ⅛ teaspoon salt, divided

Black pepper

¾ cup panko bread crumbs

¼ cup shredded Parmesan cheese

1 clove garlic, minced

¼ teaspoon dried oregano

¼ teaspoon dried sage

⅛ teaspoon red pepper flakes

1 Preheat oven to 400°F. Line 13×9-inch baking pan with foil.

2 Rub 4 tablespoons oil all over cauliflower, 1 tablespoon at at time. Sprinkle with ½ teaspoon salt and black pepper. Place in prepared baking pan; add ¼ cup water to pan. Roast 45 minutes, adding additional water if pan is dry.

3 Combine panko, Parmesan, 1 clove garlic, oregano, sage, red pepper flakes and remaining ⅛ teaspoon salt in small bowl. Stir in remaining 2 tablespoons oil. Remove pan from oven and carefully pat panko mixture all over and under cauliflower. Bake 15 minutes until panko is browned and cauliflower is tender. Cut into wedges to serve.

SERVING SUGGESTION

Serve with a kale salad and cranberry sauce. Combine 6 cups shredded kale, 1 clove minced garlic and 2 tablespoons olive oil in a large bowl; season with salt and pepper. Mix with hands, rubbing oil into kale until kale is glossy and softened slightly.

CORNMEAL-CRUSTED CAULIFLOWER STEAKS

MAKES 4 SERVINGS

½ cup cornmeal

¼ cup all-purpose flour

1 teaspoon salt

1 teaspoon dried sage

½ teaspoon garlic powder

Black pepper

½ cup milk

2 heads cauliflower

4 tablespoons butter, melted

Coleslaw and barbecue sauce (optional)

1 Preheat oven to 400°F. Line baking sheet with parchment paper.

2 Combine cornmeal, flour, salt, sage and garlic powder in shallow bowl or baking pan. Season with pepper. Pour milk into another shallow bowl.

3 Turn cauliflower stem side up on cutting board. Trim away leaves, leaving stem intact. Slice through stem into 2 or 3 slices. Trim off excess florets from two end slices, creating flat "steaks." Repeat with remaining cauliflower; reserve extra cauliflower for another use.

4 Dip cauliflower into milk to coat both sides. Place in cornmeal mixture; pat onto all sides of cauliflower. Place on prepared baking sheet. Drizzle butter evenly over cauliflower.

5 Bake 40 minutes or until cauliflower is tender. Serve with coleslaw on the side barbecue sauce for dipping, if desired.

CAULIFLOWER, SAUSAGE AND GOUDA SHEET PAN
MAKES 4 TO 6 SERVINGS

1 package (16 ounces) white mushrooms, stemmed and halved

3 tablespoons olive oil, divided

1 teaspoon salt, divided

1 head cauliflower, separated into florets and thinly sliced

¼ teaspoon chipotle chili powder

1 package (about 13 ounces) smoked sausage, cut into ¼-inch slices

2 tablespoons peach or apricot preserves

1 tablespoon Dijon mustard

½ red onion, thinly sliced

6 ounces Gouda cheese, cubed

1 Preheat oven to 400°F.

2 Place mushrooms in medium bowl. Drizzle with 1 tablespoon oil and sprinkle with ½ teaspoon salt; toss to coat. Spread on sheet pan.

3 Place cauliflower, remaining 2 tablespoons oil, ½ teaspoon salt and chipotle chili powder in same bowl; toss to coat. Spread on sheet pan with mushrooms.

4 Combine sausage, preserves and mustard in same bowl; stir until well coated. Arrange sausage over vegetables; top with onion.

5 Roast 30 minutes. Remove from oven; place cheese cubes on top of cauliflower. Bake 5 minutes or until cheese is melted and cauliflower is tender.

MEXICAN CAULIFLOWER AND BEAN SKILLET

MAKES 4 TO 6 SERVINGS

1 teaspoon olive oil

3 cups coarsely chopped cauliflower*

¾ teaspoon salt

½ medium yellow onion, chopped

1 green bell pepper, chopped

1 clove garlic, minced

1 teaspoon chili powder

¾ teaspoon ground cumin

Dash of ground red pepper

1 can (15 ounces) black beans, rinsed and drained

1 cup (4 ounces) shredded Cheddar-Jack cheese

Salsa and sour cream

See page 5 (method 3).

1 Heat oil in large nonstick skillet over medium-high heat. Add cauliflower and salt; cook and stir 5 minutes. Add onion, bell pepper, garlic, chili powder, cumin and ground red pepper; cook and stir 5 minutes or until cauliflower is tender. Add beans; cook until beans are heated through. Remove from heat.

2 Sprinkle with cheese; fold gently and let stand until melted. Serve with salsa and sour cream.

SOUPS & STEWS

COCONUT CAULIFLOWER
CREAM SOUP
70

CREAMY CAULIFLOWER BISQUE
74

LENTIL VEGETABLE STEW
72

HEARTY LENTIL STEW
76

TWO-CHEESE POTATO
AND CAULIFLOWER SOUP
78

COCONUT CAULIFLOWER CREAM SOUP

MAKES 4 TO 6 SERVINGS

1 tablespoon coconut or vegetable oil

1 medium onion, chopped

1 tablespoon minced garlic

1 tablespoon minced fresh ginger

1 teaspoon salt

1 head cauliflower, cut into florets

2 cans (about 13 ounces each) coconut milk, divided

1 cup water

1 teaspoon garam masala

½ teaspoon ground turmeric

Hot chile oil, red pepper flakes and chopped fresh cilantro (optional)

1 Heat coconut oil in large saucepan over medium-high heat. Add onion; cook and stir 5 minutes or until softened. Add garlic, ginger and salt; cook and stir 30 seconds.

2 Add cauliflower, 1 can of coconut milk, water, garam masala and turmeric. Reduce heat to medium; cover and simmer 20 minutes or until cauliflower is very tender.

3 Remove from heat. Blend soup with immersion blender until smooth.* Return saucepan to medium heat; add 1 cup additional coconut milk. Cook and stir until heated through. Add additional coconut milk, if desired, to reach desired consistency. Garnish with chili oil, red pepper flakes and cilantro.

Or blend in batches with blender or food processor, cooling to room temperature first if your appliance should not be used to blend hot liquids.

LENTIL VEGETABLE STEW

MAKES 8 SERVINGS

3 tablespoons vegetable oil
1 large onion, coarsely chopped
1 can (28 ounces) crushed tomatoes
2 cups water
1 tablespoon curry powder
1 tablespoon cider vinegar
1½ teaspoons salt
1½ teaspoons ground cumin
1½ teaspoons ground coriander
1 teaspoon ground ginger
1¼ cups dried lentils
2 cups bite-size cauliflower florets
1 cup chopped red bell pepper
1 cup chopped yellow squash

1 Heat oil in large saucepan over medium heat. Add onion; cook and stir 5 minutes or until softened. Stir in tomatoes, water, curry powder, vinegar, salt, cumin, coriander and ginger. Stir in lentils; bring to a boil. Reduce heat to medium-low; simmer 20 minutes or until lentils begin to soften.

2 Add cauliflower, bell pepper and squash; cook 20 to 30 minutes or until vegetables and lentils are tender.

CREAMY CAULIFLOWER BISQUE
MAKES 9 SERVINGS

1 head cauliflower, cut into florets

1 pound russet potatoes, peeled and cut into 1-inch cubes

3½ cups vegetable broth

1 cup chopped yellow onion

½ teaspoon dried thyme

¼ teaspoon garlic powder

⅛ teaspoon ground red pepper

1 cup evaporated milk

2 tablespoons butter

½ teaspoon salt

¼ teaspoon black pepper

1 cup (4 ounces) shredded sharp Cheddar cheese

¼ cup finely chopped fresh parsley

¼ cup finely chopped green onions

1 Combine cauliflower, potatoes, broth, onion, thyme, garlic powder and red pepper in large saucepan. Bring to a simmer over medium heat. Cover and cook 30 minutes or until potatoes and cauliflower are tender.

2 Remove from heat. Blend soup with immersion blender until smooth.* Return to medium heat. Add evaporated milk, butter, salt and black pepper; cook and stir until heated through.

3 Ladle into bowls. Top each serving with cheese, parsley and green onions.

Or blend in batches with blender or food processor, cooling to room temperature first if your appliance should not be used to blend hot liquids.

HEARTY LENTIL STEW

MAKES 6 SERVINGS

1 tablespoon olive oil

1 cup chopped onion

2 teaspoons ground cumin

¾ teaspoon ground ginger

½ teaspoon salt

3 cups vegetable broth

1 cup baby carrots, cut in half crosswise

2 cups bite-size cauliflower florets

1 cup dried lentils, rinsed and sorted

1 package (16 ounces) frozen green beans, thawed

1 can (about 14 ounces) diced tomatoes

½ cup dry-roasted peanuts

1 Heat oil in large saucepan over medium-high heat. Add onion; cook and stir 5 minutes or until softened. Add cumin, ginger and salt; cook and stir 30 seconds. Add broth, carrots, cauliflower and lentils; bring to a boil. Reduce heat to medium-low; simmer 15 minutes or until lentils begin to soften.

2 Stir in green beans and tomatoes; cook 10 minutes or until lentils and vegetables are tender. Top each serving with peanuts.

TWO-CHEESE POTATO AND CAULIFLOWER SOUP
MAKES 4 TO 6 SERVINGS

1 tablespoon butter

1 cup chopped onion

2 cloves garlic, minced

5 cups whole milk

1 pound Yukon Gold potatoes, peeled and diced

1 head cauliflower, cut into florets

1½ teaspoons salt

⅛ teaspoon ground red pepper

1½ cups (6 ounces) shredded sharp Cheddar cheese

⅓ cup crumbled blue cheese

1 Melt butter in large saucepan over medium-high heat. Add onion; cook and stir 5 minutes or until translucent. Add garlic; cook and stir 15 seconds. Add milk, potatoes, cauliflower, salt and red pepper; bring to a boil. Reduce heat to low; cover and simmer 15 minutes or until potatoes are tender. Cool slightly.

2 Remove from heat. Blend soup with immersion blender until smooth.* Return to medium heat; cook and stir just until heated through. Remove from heat; stir in cheeses until melted.

Or blend in batches with blender or food processor, cooling to room temperature first if your appliance should not be used to blend hot liquids.

SANDWICHES & PIZZAS

ROASTED CAULIFLOWER
SALAD IN PITAS
82

THAI PIZZA
92

CAULIFLOWER TARTINE
94

BARBECUE
CAULIFLOWER CALZONES
90

**GARLIC AND ONION
SHEET PAN PIZZA
84**

**CAULIFLOWER TACOS
WITH CHIPOTLE CREMA
86**

**VEGGIE-PACKED PIZZA
88**

**CHORIZO QUESADILLAS
96**

**MEDITERRANEAN ROASTED
VEGETABLE WRAPS
98**

ROASTED CAULIFLOWER SALAD IN PITAS

MAKES 6 SERVINGS

1 head cauliflower, cut into 1-inch florets

2 tablespoons olive oil

¾ teaspoon salt, divided

¼ teaspoon black pepper

½ cup mayonnaise

¼ cup plain Greek yogurt

1 teaspoon cider vinegar

1 teaspoon Dijon mustard

1 cup red grapes, halved

2 tablespoons minced fresh chives

½ cup chopped walnuts, toasted

Pita bread, cut in half, or bread

Lettuce leaves

1 Preheat oven to 425°F. Place cauliflower on sheet pan. Drizzle with oil and sprinkle with ½ teaspoon salt and pepper; toss to coat. Roast 35 to 40 minutes or until cauliflower is well browned and very tender. Cool completely.

2 Whisk mayonnaise, yogurt, vinegar, mustard and remaining ¼ teaspoon salt in large bowl. Stir in grapes, chives and cauliflower. Fold in walnuts. Serve in pita halves with lettuce.

GARLIC AND ONION SHEET PAN PIZZA
MAKES 16 SQUARES

2 teaspoons vegetable oil

1 head cauliflower

¾ cup almond flour

½ cup shredded Parmesan cheese

1½ cups (6 ounces) shredded mozzarella cheese, divided

1 teaspoon salt

1 clove garlic

½ teaspoon dried oregano

1 egg

1 cup prepared Indian butter chicken sauce*

½ sweet onion, halved and thinly sliced

1 tablespoon chopped garlic

Fresh basil leaves (optional)

Or stir ¼ whipping cream into 1 cup prepared marinara sauce in small bowl.

1 Preheat oven to 425°F. Grease sheet pan with oil or line with parchment paper.

2 Cut cauliflower into florets. Working in batches, pulse cauliflower in food processor until finely chopped (or grate into large bowl using large holes of box grater). Measure 4 cups; reserve remaining cauliflower for another use. Place cauliflower on double layer of paper towels; fold over paper towels and squeeze to remove excess moisture. Place in large bowl. Add almond flour, Parmesan, ½ cup mozzarella, salt, 1 clove garlic and oregano; mix well. Add egg; mix with hands until thoroughly blended. Turn out onto prepared sheet pan; pat into 11×14-inch rectangle. Bake 20 minutes.

3 Remove crust from oven. Spread sauce over crust to within ½ inch of edges. Sprinkle evenly with onion, chopped garlic and remaining 1 cup mozzarella. Bake 7 to 10 minutes or until cheese is bubbly and browned in spots. Garnish with basil. Cut into squares to serve.

CAULIFLOWER TACOS WITH CHIPOTLE CREMA
MAKES 8 TACOS (4 SERVINGS)

1 head cauliflower, cut into 1-inch florets

4 tablespoons olive oil, divided

1¾ teaspoons salt, divided

1 teaspoon ground cumin

½ teaspoon dried oregano

¼ teaspoon ground coriander

¼ teaspoon ground cinnamon

¼ teaspoon black pepper

1 package (8 ounces) sliced cremini mushrooms

½ cup sour cream

2 teaspoons lime juice

½ teaspoon chipotle chili powder

½ cup vegetarian refried beans

8 taco-size flour or corn tortillas

Chopped fresh cilantro

Pickled Red Onions (recipe follows) or sliced red onion

1 Preheat oven to 400°F.

2 Place cauliflower in large bowl. Add 3 tablespoons oil, 1 teaspoon salt, cumin, oregano, coriander, cinnamon and black pepper; mix well. Spread on sheet pan in single layer.

3 Roast cauliflower about 40 minutes or until browned and tender, stirring a few times. Meanwhile, toss mushrooms with remaining 1 tablespoon oil and ¼ teaspoon salt in same bowl. Spread on small baking sheet. Roast mushrooms 20 minutes or until dry and browned, stirring once.

4 For crema, combine sour cream, lime juice, chipotle chili powder and remaining ½ teaspoon salt in small bowl.

5 For each taco, spread 1 tablespoon beans over tortilla; spread 1 teaspoon crema over beans. Top with about 3 mushroom slices and ¼ cup cauliflower. Top with cilantro and red onions. Fold in half.

PICKLED RED ONIONS

Thinly slice 1 small red onion; place in large glass jar. Add ¼ cup white wine vinegar or distilled white vinegar, 2 tablespoons water, 1 teaspoon sugar and 1 teaspoon salt. Seal jar; shake well. Refrigerate at least 1 hour or up to 1 week. Makes about ½ cup.

VEGGIE-PACKED PIZZA

MAKES 6 SERVINGS

2½ cups riced cauliflower
(see page 4)

1½ cups (6 ounces)
shredded
mozzarella cheese,
divided

1 egg

4 teaspoons chopped
fresh oregano,
divided

½ cup sliced mushrooms

½ cup sliced assorted
bell peppers (red,
yellow, green and/or
a combination)

½ cup sliced red onion

2 teaspoons olive oil

3 tablespoons pasta
sauce, any flavor

Dash red pepper
flakes

1 Preheat oven to 450°F. Spray pizza pan with nonstick cooking spray. Line large baking sheet with foil.

2 Place cauliflower in medium microwavable bowl; microwave on HIGH 4 minutes. Stir; microwave on HIGH 4 minutes or until tender. Let cool slightly. Pat and squeeze cauliflower with paper towels to remove excess moisture.

3 Add 1 cup cheese, egg and 2 teaspoons oregano to cauliflower; mix well. Pat mixture into 9-inch circle on prepared pizza pan; spray with cooking spray.

4 Combine mushrooms, bell peppers and onion on prepared baking sheet. Drizzle with oil; toss to coat.

5 Roast vegetables 14 to 15 minutes or until tender. Bake cauliflower crust during last 10 to 12 minutes of cooking time or until crust is golden brown around edges.

6 Spread pasta sauce over crust; top with roasted vegetables and remaining ½ cup cheese. Bake 6 to 7 minutes or just until cheese is melted. Sprinkle with remaining 2 teaspoons oregano and red pepper flakes. Cut into 6 wedges.

BARBECUE CAULIFLOWER CALZONES

MAKES 4 SERVINGS

1 head cauliflower, cut into florets and thinly sliced

2 tablespoons olive oil

Salt and black pepper

¾ cup barbecue sauce

1 can (about 13 ounces) pizza dough

½ yellow onion, chopped

1 cup (4 ounces) shredded mozzarella cheese

Ranch or blue cheese dressing

1 Preheat oven to 400°F.

2 Spread cauliflower on sheet pan; drizzle with oil and season lightly with salt and pepper. Toss to coat; spread in single layer.

3 Roast 30 minutes or until cauliflower is browned and very tender, stirring once. Transfer to medium bowl; stir in barbecue sauce.

4 Unroll pizza dough onto cutting board. Stretch into 11×17-inch rectangle; cut into quarters. Place one fourth of onion on half of each piece of dough. Top with one fourth of cauliflower and ¼ cup cheese. Bring dough over filling; roll and pinch edges to seal. Place on baking sheet. Spray with nonstick cooking spray or brush with oil to help crust brown.

5 Bake 10 minutes or until golden brown. Serve with ranch dressing.

THAI PIZZA
MAKES 8 SERVINGS

CRUST

2	teaspoons vegetable oil
1	head cauliflower
¾	cup almond flour
½	cup shredded Parmesan cheese
½	cup (2 ounces) shredded mozzarella cheese
1	teaspoon salt
1	egg

TOPPINGS

½	cup prepared Thai peanut sauce
½	cup thinly sliced red onion
1	carrot, chopped
1	cup (4 ounces) shredded mozzarella cheese
1	cup coleslaw mix
¼	cup chopped fresh cilantro
1	tablespoon lime juice
⅛	teaspoon salt
3	tablespoons chopped roasted unsalted peanuts

1 Preheat oven to 425°F. Grease sheet pan with oil or line with parchment paper.

2 Cut cauliflower into florets. Working in batches, pulse cauliflower in food processor until finely chopped (or grate into large bowl using large holes of box grater). Measure 4 cups; reserve remaining cauliflower for another use. Place cauliflower on double layer of paper towels; fold over paper towels and squeeze to remove excess moisture. Place in large bowl. Add almond flour, Parmesan, ½ cup mozzarella and 1 teaspoon salt; mix well. Add egg; mix with hands until thoroughly blended. Turn out onto prepared sheet pan; pat into 11-inch circle. Bake 20 minutes.

3 Remove crust from oven. Spread sauce over crust to within ½ inch of edge. Sprinkle with onion, carrot and 1 cup mozzarella. Bake 7 to 10 minutes or until cheese is melted and browned in spots.

4 Meanwhile, combine coleslaw mix, cilantro, lime juice and ⅛ teaspoon salt in small bowl. Stir in peanuts. Sprinkle over pizza; cut into wedges to serve.

CAULIFLOWER TARTINE

MAKES 4 SERVINGS

¼ cup plus
    2 tablespoons
    water, divided

2 tablespoons sugar

1½ teaspoons salt,
    divided

1 cup thinly sliced red
    onion

¾ cup white vinegar

1 tablespoon olive oil

2 cups thinly sliced
    cauliflower florets

1 clove garlic, minced

½ teaspoon cumin seeds

¼ teaspoon dried thyme

Black pepper

Mayonnaise and Dijon
    mustard

4 large or 8 small whole
    grain or French
    bread slices, toasted

8 ounces Brie cheese,
    thinly sliced

Microgreens, sprouts
    or baby arugula

2 tablespoons pine nuts,
    toasted

1 Bring water, sugar and 1 teaspoon salt to a simmer in small saucepan; cook and stir until sugar and salt are dissolved. Pour into medium jar or bowl; stir in onions and vinegar. Add enough additional water to cover, if needed. Let stand until ready to use; onions can be made a few days in advance.

2 Heat oil in medium skillet over medium-high heat. Add cauliflower; cook and stir 5 minutes or until browned. Add garlic, cumin, thyme, remaining ½ teaspoon salt and pepper; cook and stir 30 seconds. Add remaining 2 tablespoons water; cook and stir 5 minutes or until water is absorbed and cauliflower is crisp-tender.

3 Spread mayonnaise and mustard over each slice of bread. Top with Brie, cauliflower, greens, pickled onions and pine nuts.

CHORIZO QUESADILLAS

MAKES 6 SERVINGS

1 package (9 ounces) chorizo

1 cup coarsely chopped cauliflower*

1 small onion, finely chopped

12 (6-inch) flour tortillas

1½ cups (6 ounces) chihuahua cheese

6 teaspoons vegetable oil

Salsa, guacamole and sour cream

See page 5 (method 3).

1 Heat medium skillet over medium-high heat. Add chorizo, cauliflower and onion; cook and stir 10 to 12 minutes or until cauliflower is tender. Transfer to bowl. Wipe out skillet.

2 Spread ¼ cup chorizo mixture onto each of 4 tortillas. Top with ¼ cup cheese and remaining tortillas.

3 Heat 1 teaspoon oil in same skillet over medium-high heat. Add one quesadilla; cook 2 to 3 minutes per side or until well browned and cheese is melted. Repeat with remaining oil and quesadillas. Cut into wedges; serve with salsa, guacamole and sour cream.

NOTE

To keep cooked quesadillas warm, arrange on a baking sheet and place in a preheated 200°F oven until all the quesadillas are cooked and ready to serve.

MEDITERRANEAN ROASTED VEGETABLE WRAPS
MAKES 4 SERVINGS

1 head cauliflower, cut into 1-inch florets

4 tablespoons olive oil, divided

2 teaspoons ras el hanout, 7-spice blend, shawarma blend or za'atar

1 teaspoon salt, divided

1 zucchini, quartered lengthwise and cut into ¼-inch pieces

1 yellow squash, quartered lengthwise and cut into ¼-inch pieces

½ red onion, thinly sliced

¼ cup red pepper sauce (avjar)

4 large thin pitas or lavash (10 inches)

4 ounces feta cheese, crumbled

1 cup chickpeas

¼ cup diced tomatoes

¼ cup minced fresh parsley

¼ cup diced cucumber (optional)

2 teaspoons vegetable oil

1 Preheat oven to 400°F. Combine cauliflower, 2 tablespoons olive oil, ras el hanout and ½ teaspoon salt in large bowl; toss to coat. Spread on half of sheet pan. Combine zucchini, yellow squash, onion, remaining 2 tablespoons olive oil and ½ teaspoon salt in same bowl; toss to coat. Spread on other side of sheet pan. Roast 25 minutes or until vegetables are browned and tender, stirring once. Remove from oven; cool slightly.

2 Spread 1 tablespoon red pepper sauce on one pita. Top with one fourth of vegetables, feta, chickpeas, tomatoes, parsley and cucumber, if desired. Fold two sides over filling; roll up into burrito shape. Repeat with remaining ingredients.

3 Heat 1 teaspoon vegetable oil in large skillet over medium-high heat. Add two wraps, seam sides down; cook 1 minute or until browned. Turn and cook other side until browned. Repeat with remaining vegetable oil and wraps. Cut in half to serve.

SALADS & SIDES

CAULIFLOWER CHOPPED SALAD
102

CHEESY CAULIFLOWER
114

CAULIFLOWER HASH BROWNS
116

PORK SALAD TOSS WITH BALSAMIC GLAZE
118

CAULIFLOWER WITH ONION BUTTER
120

QUICK MASHED POTATOES WITH CAULIFLOWER
122

BARLEY VEGETABLE CASSEROLE
124

CAULIFLOWER CHOPPED SALAD
MAKES 8 SERVINGS

½ cup red wine vinegar

¼ cup olive oil

1 teaspoon salt

1 teaspoon honey

1 teaspoon Dijon mustard

½ teaspoon dried oregano

1 clove garlic, minced

¼ teaspoon black pepper

2 cups small cauliflower florets (½ inch)

1 head iceberg lettuce, chopped

1 container (4 ounces) crumbled blue cheese

1 pint grape tomatoes, halved *or* 1 cup finely chopped tomatoes

½ cup finely chopped red onion

2 green onions, finely chopped

1 avocado, diced

1 For cauliflower, whisk vinegar, oil, salt, honey, mustard, oregano, garlic and pepper in medium bowl. Add cauliflower; stir to coat. Cover and refrigerate several hours or overnight.

2 For salad, combine lettuce, blue cheese, tomatoes, red onion and green onions in large bowl; toss to coat. Remove cauliflower from marinade using slotted spoon; place on salad. Whisk marinade; pour over salad and toss to coat. Top with avocado; mix gently.

CAULIFLOWER AND LEEK GRATIN

MAKES 6 TO 8 SERVINGS

4 tablespoons butter, divided

2 large leeks, sliced

2 tablespoons minced garlic

1 head cauliflower, cut into 1-inch florets

2 cups milk

3 eggs

2 teaspoons salt

¼ teaspoon white pepper

2 to 3 slices dense day-old white bread, such as French or Italian

¼ cup grated Parmesan cheese

1 Preheat oven to 375°F. Spray shallow 2½-quart baking dish with nonstick cooking spray.

2 Melt 2 tablespoons butter in large skillet over medium heat. Add leeks and garlic; cook and stir 8 to 10 minutes or until leeks are softened. Remove from heat.

3 Layer half of cauliflower in prepared baking dish; top with half of leek mixture. Repeat layers. Whisk milk, eggs, salt and pepper in medium bowl until well blended; pour evenly over vegetables.

4 Tear bread slices into 1-inch pieces. Place in food processor or blender; pulse until fine crumbs form. Measure ¾ cup crumbs; place in small bowl. Stir in Parmesan. Melt remaining 2 tablespoons butter; stir into crumb mixture. Sprinkle crumb mixture evenly over vegetables.

5 Bake 1 hour or until top is golden brown and cauliflower is tender. Let stand 5 to 10 minutes before serving.

ROASTED CURRIED CAULIFLOWER AND BRUSSELS SPROUTS

MAKES 6 TO 8 SERVINGS

2 pounds cauliflower florets

¾ pound brussels sprouts, cut in half lengthwise

⅓ cup olive oil

2½ tablespoons curry powder

½ teaspoon salt

½ teaspoon black pepper

½ cup chopped fresh cilantro

1 Preheat oven to 400°F. Spray sheet pan with nonstick cooking spray.

2 Combine cauliflower, brussels sprouts and oil in large bowl; toss to coat. Sprinkle with curry powder, salt and pepper; toss to coat. Spread vegetables in single layer on prepared pan.

3 Roast 20 to 25 minutes or until golden brown and tender, stirring once.

4 Sprinkle with cilantro; toss until blended.

CAULIFLOWER PICNIC SALAD
MAKES 6 SERVINGS

2 teaspoons salt

1 head cauliflower, cut into 1-inch florets

¾ cup mayonnaise

1 tablespoon yellow mustard

2 tablespoons minced fresh parsley

⅓ cup chopped dill pickle

⅓ cup minced red onion

2 hard-cooked eggs, chopped

   Salt and black pepper

1 Fill large saucepan with 1 inch of water. Bring to a simmer over medium-high heat; stir in 2 teaspoons salt. Add cauliflower; reduce heat to medium. Cover and cook 5 to 7 minutes or until cauliflower is fork-tender but not mushy. Drain and cool slightly.

2 Whisk mayonnaise, mustard and parsley in large bowl. Stir in pickle and onion. Gently fold in cauliflower and eggs. Season with salt and pepper, if desired. Refrigerate until ready to serve.

NOTE

For perfect hard-cooked eggs, bring a medium saucepan of water to a boil. Gently add the eggs with slotted spoon. Reduce heat to maintain a gentle boil; cook 12 minutes. Meanwhile, prepare an ice bath. Drain eggs and place them in the ice bath. Cool 10 minutes and then peel.

CAULIFLOWER POTATO PANCAKES

MAKES 12 PANCAKES

1½ cups cubed Yukon Gold potatoes

3 cups coarsely chopped cauliflower

⅓ cup whole wheat flour

1 egg

1 egg white

1 tablespoon chopped fresh chives, plus additional for garnish

1 teaspoon baking powder

½ teaspoon salt

3 teaspoons vegetable oil

Sour cream (optional)

1 Bring large saucepan of water to a boil. Add potatoes and cauliflower; reduce heat. Simmer 10 minutes or until fork-tender. Drain potatoes and cauliflower. Let stand 5 to 10 minutes or until cool enough to handle.

2 Gently mash potatoes and cauliflower in large bowl. Add flour, egg, egg white, 1 tablespoon chives, baking powder and salt; mix well.

3 Heat 1 teaspoon oil in large nonstick skillet over medium heat. Drop ¼ cupfuls of potato mixture into skillet; flatten slightly. Cook 5 to 7 minutes per side or until golden brown. Repeat with remaining oil and potato mixture.

4 Serve with sour cream, if desired. Garnish with additional chives.

TWICE-BAKED LOADED CAULIFLOWER

MAKES 4 TO 6 SERVINGS

2 heads cauliflower, cut into florets

2 tablespoons vegetable or olive oil

1 teaspoon salt

¼ cup (½ stick) butter, cut into pieces

¼ cup milk

½ cup chopped green onions, divided

1 cup (4 ounces) shredded Cheddar cheese, divided

4 ounces bacon, crisp cooked and crumbled

½ cup chopped tomatoes

Sour cream

1 Preheat oven to 425°F. Divide cauliflower between two 13×9-inch baking pans. Drizzle each with 1 tablespoon oil and sprinkle each with ½ teaspoon salt. Roast 40 minutes, stirring cauliflower and rotating pans once. *Reduce oven temperature to 375°F.*

2 Transfer cauliflower to food processor; add butter and milk. Process 1 to 2 minutes until very smooth and fluffy. Stir in half of green onions and ½ cup cheese. Divide mixture among 4 to 6 ramekins. Sprinkle with remaining ½ cup cheese and bacon.

3 Bake 10 to 15 minutes or until cheese is melted and browned around edge and cauliflower is heated through. Top with remaining green onions, tomatoes and sour cream.

CHEESY CAULIFLOWER
MAKES 8 TO 10 SERVINGS

2½ teaspoons salt, divided

3 pounds cauliflower florets (2 heads)

5 tablespoons butter

1 cup finely chopped onion

6 tablespoons all-purpose flour

¼ teaspoon dry mustard

2 cups milk

2 cups (about 8 ounces) shredded sharp Cheddar cheese

½ teaspoon ground black pepper

1 Fill large saucepan with 1 inch of water. Bring to a simmer over medium-high heat; stir in 2 teaspoons salt. Add cauliflower; cover and cook 10 minutes or until cauliflower is fork-tender but not mushy. Drain and return to saucepan.

2 Meanwhile, melt butter in medium saucepan over medium-high heat. Add onion; cook and stir 2 to 3 minutes or until slightly softened. Whisk in flour and mustard; cook and stir 3 minutes. Gradually whisk in milk until smooth. Bring to boil and cook until thickened, whisking constantly. Stir in cheese, remaining ½ teaspoon salt and black pepper. Whisk until smooth.

3 Pour cheese sauce over cauliflower; stir until well coated.

CAULIFLOWER HASH BROWNS

MAKES 8 SERVINGS

4 slices bacon, coarsely chopped

1 package (about 12 ounces) frozen cauliflower rice

½ cup finely chopped onion

½ cup finely chopped red and/or green bell pepper

1 egg

⅓ cup all-purpose flour or almond flour

½ cup (2 ounces) shredded Cheddar cheese

1 tablespoon minced fresh chives

1 teaspoon salt

½ teaspoon black pepper

1 Cook bacon in medium skillet over medium heat 5 to 7 minutes or until crisp. Remove from skillet with slotted spoon; drain on paper towel-lined plate.

2 Spray baking sheet with nonstick cooking spray. Place cauliflower in large bowl. Add bacon, onion, bell pepper, egg, flour, cheese, chives, salt and black pepper; mix well. Shape mixture into 8 patties; place on prepared baking sheet. Freeze 30 minutes.

3 Preheat oven to 375°F. Bake patties about 15 minutes or until browned and heated through.

PORK SALAD TOSS WITH BALSAMIC GLAZE

MAKES 4 SERVINGS

½ cup balsamic vinegar

4 ounces thinly sliced cooked pork tenderloin (about ½ cup)

2 cups bite-size cauliflower florets

1 medium red bell pepper, cored and thinly sliced

1 cup snow peas

1 cup vegetable broth

4 cups mixed salad greens

2 tablespoons roasted sunflower seeds

Salt and black pepper (optional)

1 Boil vinegar in small saucepan over medium-high heat about 8 minutes or until liquid is reduced by two-thirds and becomes syrupy;* set aside.

2 Place pork, cauliflower, bell pepper, snow peas and broth in medium skillet. Cover and cook over medium heat 10 minutes or until vegetables are tender, stirring every 5 minutes. Drain pork and vegetables.

3 Divide greens among four salad bowls; top with pork and vegetables. Drizzle with balsamic glaze; sprinkle with sunflower seeds. Season with salt and black pepper, if desired.

Watch vinegar carefully, because reduction will occur very quickly towards the end of cooking time. If it overcooks, the vinegar will have an unpleasant flavor.

CAULIFLOWER WITH ONION BUTTER

MAKES 6 SERVINGS

½ cup (1 stick) butter, divided

1 cup diced onion

1 head cauliflower, cut into 1-inch florets

½ cup water

Salt and black pepper

1 Melt ¼ cup butter in medium skillet over medium heat. Add onion; cook about 20 minutes or until onion is deep golden brown, stirring occasionally.

2 Meanwhile, place cauliflower and water in microwavable bowl. Cover and microwave on HIGH 8 minutes or until crisp-tender; drain.

3 Add remaining ¼ cup butter to skillet with onion; cook and stir until butter is melted. Pour over cooked cauliflower; season with salt and pepper. Serve immediately.

QUICK MASHED POTATOES WITH CAULIFLOWER

MAKES 4 SERVINGS

16 ounces russet potatoes, peeled and cut into 2-inch chunks

1 head cauliflower, cut into florets

¼ cup water

2 tablespoons butter

2 cloves garlic, minced

½ teaspoon salt

¼ teaspoon black pepper

2 tablespoons minced fresh chives

1 Place potatoes in medium saucepan; cover with water. Cover; bring to a boil. Reduce heat; simmer 15 minutes or until tender. Drain.

2 Meanwhile, place cauliflower and ¼ cup water in microwavable dish. Cover and microwave on HIGH 5 minutes or until just tender. Drain.

3 Combine potatoes and cauliflower in large bowl. Mash with potato masher to desired consistency. Add butter, garlic, salt and pepper; mix well. Sprinkle with chives.

BARLEY VEGETABLE CASSEROLE

MAKES 4 SERVINGS

3 tablespoons butter, divided

1 cup chopped onion

⅔ cup uncooked barley (not quick-cooking)

2 cups bite-size cauliflower florets

1 cup broccoli florets

2 carrots, sliced

2¼ cups vegetable broth

½ teaspoon salt

½ teaspoon garlic powder

¼ teaspoon black pepper

Additional salt and black pepper

1 Preheat oven to 350°F. Spray 1-quart baking dish with nonstick cooking spray.

2 Melt 1 tablespoon butter in medium nonstick skillet. Add onion and barley; cook and stir 3 minutes or until barley is lightly browned. Transfer to prepared baking dish. Add cauliflower, broccoli, carrots, broth, ½ teaspoon salt, garlic powder and ¼ teaspoon pepper; mix well.

3 Cover and bake 50 minutes or until barley is tender and most of liquid is absorbed, stirring several times during baking. Stir in remaining 2 tablespoons butter; season with additional salt and pepper, if desired. Let stand 5 minutes before serving.

QUICK CREAMED CAULIFLOWER
MAKES 3 SERVINGS

1 package (10 ounces) frozen cauliflower florets

½ cup vegetable broth

½ cup evaporated milk

2 tablespoons all-purpose flour

Salt and black pepper

Smoked or regular paprika (optional)

1 Combine cauliflower and broth in saucepan. Cover and simmer 10 to 12 minutes or until cauliflower is tender.

2 Whisk evaporated milk and flour in small bowl until well blended; stir into saucepan. Cook and stir until sauce simmers and bubbles. Sprinkle with salt, pepper and paprika, if desired, before serving.

ROASTED CAULIFLOWER WITH HERBED PEPPER SAUCE

MAKES 4 SERVINGS

5 cups cauliflower florets (about 1¼ pounds)

1 tablespoon olive oil

1 small red bell pepper, cut into quarters

Salt and black pepper

2 tablespoons water

3 large tomatoes, peeled, seeded and coarsely chopped

2 to 3 teaspoons chopped fresh tarragon

1 teaspoon chopped fresh parsley

1 tablespoon butter

1 clove garlic, minced

½ cup panko bread crumbs

1 Preheat oven to 450°F.

2 Toss cauliflower with oil in large bowl; place cauliflower and bell pepper in single layer on sheet pan. Season with salt and black pepper; sprinkle with 2 tablespoons water.

3 Bake 15 minutes. *Reduce oven temperature to 425°F.*

4 Bake 25 minutes or until cauliflower is tender and golden brown and bell pepper skin is blistered. Remove bell pepper pieces to plate and transfer cauliflower to 11×7-inch baking dish. *Reduce oven temperature to 400°F.*

5 Remove and discard skin from bell pepper. Place tomatoes and bell pepper in food processor; process until smooth. Add tarragon and parsley; process until blended. Season with salt and black pepper. Pour tomato sauce over cauliflower.

6 Melt 1 tablespoon butter in small saucepan over medium heat. Add garlic; cook and stir 30 seconds. Stir in panko. Sprinkle over cauliflower; bake 10 minutes.

CAULIFLOWER MASH

MAKES 6 SERVINGS

1 teaspoon salt, plus additional for serving

2 heads cauliflower, cut into florets

1 tablespoon butter

1 tablespoon half-and-half or milk

1 Fill large saucepan with 2 inches of water; stir in 1 teaspoon salt. Add cauliflower; cover and cook over medium heat 20 to 25 minutes or until cauliflower is very tender and falling apart. Drain well.

2 Place cauliflower in food processor or blender; process until almost smooth. Add butter; process until smooth, adding half-and-half as needed to reach desired consistency. Season with additional salt, if desired.

CAULIFLOWER CAPRESE SALAD

MAKES 8 SERVINGS

1 head cauliflower, cut into florets and thinly sliced

¾ cup balsamic vinegar

½ cup olive oil

1 teaspoon salt

1 teaspoon sugar

1 clove garlic, minced

1 teaspoon Italian seasoning

1 container (8 ounces) pearl-shaped fresh mozzarella cheese *or* 1 (8-ounce) ball fresh mozzarella, sliced or chopped

2 cups chopped fresh tomatoes *or* 1 pint grape tomatoes, halved

¼ cup shredded fresh basil

1 Place cauliflower in large resealable food storage bag or large bowl. Add vinegar, oil, salt, sugar, garlic and Italian seasoning. Seal bag; shake to coat. Marinate in refrigerator 8 hours or overnight.

2 Pour cauliflower and marinade into large bowl. Stir in cheese, tomatoes and basil.

NOTE

Turn leftovers into a great entrée. Cook pasta (any shape) according to package directions. Drain and immediately toss with leftover caprese salad. Serve warm or at room temperature.

SPICY PICKLED RELISH

MAKES 6 CUPS

8   serrano or jalapeño peppers, thinly sliced

2   banana peppers, sliced

3   cups cauliflower florets

2   carrots, thinly sliced

½   cup salt

1½   cups olive oil

1½   cups white vinegar

3   cloves garlic, thinly sliced

1   teaspoon dried oregano

1 Layer peppers, cauliflower and carrots in large jar or large covered bowl or container. Sprinkle with salt; fill with water to cover. Cover and refrigerate overnight.

2 Drain and thoroughly rinse vegetables under cold water. Return vegetables to jar. Pour oil and vinegar over vegetables. Add garlic and oregano; cover and shake or stir until well coated. Marinate in refrigerator at least 8 hours.

BROCCOLI AND CAULIFLOWER SALAD

MAKES 8 SERVINGS

1 package (about 12 ounces) bacon, chopped

2 cups mayonnaise

¼ cup sugar

¼ cup white or apple cider vinegar

4 cups chopped raw broccoli

4 cups coarsely chopped raw cauliflower

1½ cups (6 ounces) shredded Cheddar cheese

1 cup chopped red onion

1 cup dried cranberries or raisins (optional)

½ cup sunflower seeds (optional)

Salt and black pepper

1 Cook bacon in large skillet over medium heat until crisp. Remove from skillet with slotted spoon; drain on paper towel-lined plate.

2 Whisk mayonnaise, sugar and vinegar in large bowl. Stir in broccoli, cauliflower, cheese, onion and cranberries, if desired; mix well. Fold in bacon and sunflower seeds, if desired. Season with salt and pepper.

3 Serve immediately or cover and refrigerate until ready to serve.

QUINOA AND CAULIFLOWER TACO SALAD
MAKES 8 SERVINGS

¾ cup uncooked quinoa

1½ cups water

4 cloves garlic, minced, divided

1 tablespoon chili powder

1½ teaspoons salt, divided

1¼ teaspoons ground cumin, divided

½ teaspoon dried oregano

¼ cup plus 1 teaspoon olive oil, divided

4 cups coarsely chopped cauliflower

Juice of 1 lime

Salt and black pepper

4 to 6 cups shredded iceberg lettuce

Diced tomatoes, sliced avocado, toasted pepitas, crumbled shredded Cheddar cheese, crispy tortilla strips and crema

1 Rinse quinoa in fine-mesh strainer under cold water. Place in medium saucepan. Add 1½ cups water, 3 cloves garlic, chili powder, 1 teaspoon salt, 1 teaspoon cumin and oregano. Bring to a boil over medium-high heat. Reduce heat to low; cover and simmer 15 minutes or until quinoa is tender and most of water is absorbed.

2 Meanwhile, heat 1 teaspoon oil in large nonstick skillet over medium-high heat. Add cauliflower and remaining ½ teaspoon salt; cook and stir 10 minutes or until tender and browned. Add quinoa to cauliflower; cook and stir until well blended.

3 For dressing, whisk remaining ¼ cup olive oil, ¼ teaspoon cumin and lime juice in medium bowl. Season with salt and pepper.

4 Arrange lettuce on large serving platter. Top with quinoa mixture, tomatoes, avocado, cheese, pepitas and tortilla strips in large serving bowl. Serve with crema and dressing.

SNACKS

FRIED CAULIFLOWER WITH
GARLIC TAHINI SAUCE
142

BUFFALO CAULIFLOWER BITES
148

GARLIC "BREAD" STICKS
150

CAULIFLOWER SOCCA
144

CAULIFLOWER HUMMUS
146

ROASTED CAULIFLOWER
RAREBIT
152

CRISPY RANCH
CAULIFLOWER BITES
154

FRIED CAULIFLOWER WITH GARLIC TAHINI SAUCE
MAKES 8 SERVINGS

SAUCE

½ cup tahini

¼ cup plain Greek yogurt

2 tablespoons lemon juice

2 cloves garlic, minced

¼ teaspoon salt

6 tablespoons water

1 tablespoon minced fresh parsley

CAULIFLOWER

1 cup all-purpose flour

1½ teaspoons salt, divided

Pinch black pepper

4 eggs

¼ cup water

2 cups panko bread crumbs

1 teaspoon ground cumin

1 teaspoon garlic powder

¼ teaspoon ground nutmeg

1 large head cauliflower (2½ pounds), cut into 1-inch florets

1 quart vegetable oil

1 For sauce, whisk tahini, yogurt, lemon juice, garlic and ¼ teaspoon salt in medium bowl. Whisk in enough water in thin steady stream until sauce is thinned to desired consistency. Stir in parsley.

2 For cauliflower, whisk flour, ½ teaspoon salt and pepper in large bowl. Whisk eggs and ¼ cup water in medium bowl. Combine panko, remaining 1 teaspoon salt, cumin, garlic powder and nutmeg in large bowl. Toss cauliflower in flour mixture to coat; tap off excess. Dip in egg mixture, letting excess drip back into bowl. Roll in panko mixture to coat. Place breaded cauliflower on sheet pan.

3 Line another sheet pan with three layers of paper towels. Place oil in large deep saucepan. Clip deep-fry or candy thermometer to side of pan. Heat over medium-high heat to 350°F; adjust heat to maintain temperature between batches. Add cauliflower in batches; cook 4 minutes, stirring once or twice. Drain on prepared sheet pan. Serve warm with sauce.

CAULIFLOWER SOCCA
MAKES 8 SERVINGS

2 cups chickpea flour

1¾ teaspoons salt

¼ teaspoon black pepper

2 cups water

½ cup olive oil, divided

1½ cups finely chopped cauliflower

1 can (15 ounces) chickpeas, rinsed and drained

2 tablespoons chopped fresh cilantro or parsley

1 Thoroughly whisk chickpea flour, salt and pepper in large bowl to remove any lumps. Whisk in water and ¼ cup oil. Let stand at room temperature 30 minutes.

2 Meanwhile, preheat oven to 450°F. Place 12-inch cast iron skillet in oven to preheat 10 minutes. Pour remaining ¼ cup oil into hot skillet. Add cauliflower and chickpeas. Bake 10 minutes.

3 Whisk cilantro into batter; pour batter over cauliflower and chickpeas in skillet. Bake 15 minutes or until edge is lightly browned, top is firm and toothpick inserted into center comes out with moist crumbs. Cut into wedges; serve warm or at room temperature.

CAULIFLOWER HUMMUS

MAKES 3 CUPS

2½ teaspoons salt, divided

1 head cauliflower, cut into 1-inch florets

½ clove garlic

¾ cup tahini

2 tablespoons lemon juice

Olive oil and paprika for serving

Sliced raw fennel and/or bell pepper strips for dipping

1 Fill large saucepan with 1 inch of water. Bring to a simmer over medium-high heat; stir in 2 teaspoons salt. Add cauliflower; reduce heat to medium. Cover and cook about 10 minutes or until cauliflower is very tender. Drain and cool slightly.

2 Process cauliflower, garlic and remaining ½ teaspoon salt in food processor 1 minute. Scrape side of bowl. With motor running, add tahini and lemon juice; process 2 minutes until very smooth and fluffy. Transfer hummus to bowl; drizzle with oil and sprinkle with paprika, if desired. Serve with fennel and/or bell pepper strips.

BUFFALO CAULIFLOWER BITES

MAKES 8 SERVINGS

¾ cup all-purpose flour

¼ cup cornstarch

1 teaspoon salt

½ teaspoon garlic powder

¼ teaspoon black pepper

1 cup water

1 large head cauliflower (2½ pounds), cut into 1-inch florets

½ cup hot pepper sauce

¼ cup (½ stick) butter, melted

Blue cheese or ranch dressing and celery sticks for serving

1 Preheat oven to 450°F. Line sheet pan with foil; spray with nonstick cooking spray.

2 Whisk flour, cornstarch, salt, garlic powder and black pepper in large bowl. Whisk in water until smooth and well blended. Add cauliflower to batter in batches; stir to coat. Arrange on prepared sheet pan.

3 Bake 20 minutes or until lightly browned. Combine hot pepper sauce and butter in small bowl. Pour over cauliflower; toss until well blended. Bake 5 minutes; stir. Bake 5 minutes more or until cauliflower is glazed and crisp. Serve with blue cheese and celery sticks.

GARLIC "BREAD" STICKS
MAKES ABOUT 21 STICKS

1 tablespoon vegetable oil

1 medium head cauliflower, finely chopped and squeezed dry

1 cup (4 ounces) shredded mozzarella cheese

1 cup shredded Parmesan cheese, divided

¾ cup almond flour

2 cloves garlic, minced

½ teaspoon Italian seasoning

1 teaspoon salt

1 egg

Warm marinara sauce or pizza sauce

1 Preheat oven to 425°F. Grease sheet pan with vegetable oil or line with parchment paper.

2 Combine cauliflower, mozzarella, ½ cup Parmesan, almond flour, garlic, Italian seasoning, salt and egg in large bowl; mix well. Pat into 12×10-inch rectangle on prepared sheet pan.

3 Bake 30 minutes or until well browned and edges are crispy. Sprinkle with remaining ½ cup Parmesan. Bake 10 minutes or until cheese is melted. Cut lengthwise into thirds; cut crosswise into strips. Serve with sauce for dipping.

ROASTED CAULIFLOWER RAREBIT

MAKES 4 TO 6 SERVINGS (1¼ CUPS SAUCE)

1 large head cauliflower (about 2½ pounds), trimmed and cut into ½-inch florets

2 tablespoons vegetable oil, divided

½ teaspoon salt, divided

½ teaspoon black pepper

2 medium shallots, finely chopped

2 teaspoons all-purpose flour

½ cup Irish ale

1 tablespoon spicy brown mustard

1 tablespoon Worcestershire sauce

1½ cups (6 ounces) shredded Cheddar cheese

1 Preheat oven to 450°F. Line large baking sheet with foil.

2 Combine cauliflower, 1 tablespoon oil, ¼ teaspoon salt and pepper in medium bowl; toss to coat. Spread in single layer on prepared baking sheet.

3 Bake about 30 minutes or until tender and lightly browned, stirring once.

4 Meanwhile for sauce, heat remaining 1 tablespoon oil in medium saucepan over medium heat. Add shallots; cook and stir 3 to 4 minutes or until tender. Add flour and remaining ¼ teaspoon salt; cook and stir 1 minute. Add ale, mustard and Worcestershire sauce; bring to a simmer over medium-high heat. Reduce heat to medium-low; add cheese by ¼ cupfuls, stirring until cheese is melted before adding next addition. Cover and keep warm over low heat, stirring occasionally.

5 Transfer roasted cauliflower to large serving bowl; top with cheese sauce. Serve immediately.

CRISPY RANCH CAULIFLOWER BITES

MAKES 6 SERVINGS

1 cup ranch dressing, plus additional for serving

¼ cup milk

2 cups panko bread crumbs

1 small head cauliflower, cut into 1-inch florets

Barbecue sauce and/or ketchup

1 Preheat oven to 375°F. Line baking sheet with foil; spray foil with nonstick cooking spray.

2 Whisk ranch dressing and milk in medium bowl. Spread panko in shallow dish. Dip cauliflower in ranch dressing; shake off excess. Roll in panko to coat. Place on prepared baking sheet. Spray with cooking spray.

3 Bake 15 to 17 minutes or until golden brown and tender. Serve with barbecue sauce or ketchup.

BROCCOLI

LEFTOVER MASHED POTATO
AND BROCCOLI PUFFS
158

CHEESY BROCCOLI AND
BACON QUINOA
160

BROCCOLI CHEESE SOUP
162

GREEN CURRY WITH TOFU
164

BROCCOLI AND CHEESE
166

PASTA WITH BROCCOLI PESTO
168

VEGGIE-PACKED SPAGHETTI
AND MEATBALLS
170

WHOLE WHEAT PENNE WITH
BROCCOLI AND SAUSAGE
184

MACARONI AND CHEESE
WITH BROCCOLI
186

LEFTOVER MASHED POTATO AND BROCCOLI PUFFS
MAKES 18 PUFFS

1 cup prepared mashed potatoes

½ cup finely chopped broccoli

2 egg whites

4 tablespoons shredded Parmesan cheese, divided

1 Preheat oven to 400°F. Spray 18 mini (1¾-inch) muffin cups with nonstick cooking spray.

2 Combine mashed potatoes, broccoli, egg whites and 2 tablespoons cheese in large bowl; mix well. Spoon evenly into prepared muffin cups. Sprinkle with remaining 2 tablespoons cheese.

3 Bake 20 to 23 minutes or until golden brown. To remove from pan, gently run knife around edges and lift out with fork. Serve warm.

CHEESY BROCCOLI AND BACON QUINOA

MAKES 4 SERVINGS

1 cup tri-color uncooked quinoa

2 cups chicken broth

½ teaspoon dried thyme

2 cups broccoli florets

1 cup (4 ounces) shredded sharp Cheddar cheese

¼ cup cooked diced bacon or bacon bits

¼ teaspoon salt

1 Place quinoa in fine-mesh strainer; rinse well under cold water.

2 Combine quinoa, broth, thyme and broccoli in medium saucepan; bring to a boil over high heat. Reduce heat to low; cover and simmer 15 to 20 minutes or until quinoa is tender and broth is absorbed.

3 Remove from heat. Stir in cheese, bacon and salt.

BROCCOLI CHEESE SOUP

MAKES 4 TO 6 SERVINGS

6 tablespoons (¾ stick) butter

1 cup chopped onion

1 clove garlic, minced

¼ cup all-purpose flour

2 cups vegetable broth

2 cups milk

1½ teaspoons Dijon mustard

½ teaspoon salt

¼ teaspoon ground nutmeg

¼ teaspoon black pepper

⅛ teaspoon hot pepper sauce

1 package (16 ounces) frozen broccoli (5 cups)

2 carrots, shredded (1 cup)

6 ounces pasteurized process cheese product, cubed

1 cup (4 ounces) shredded sharp Cheddar cheese, plus additional for garnish

1 Melt butter in large saucepan or Dutch oven over medium-low heat. Add onion; cook and stir 8 minutes or until softened. Add garlic; cook and stir 1 minute. Increase heat to medium. Whisk in flour until smooth; cook and stir 3 minutes without browning.

2 Gradually whisk in broth and milk. Add mustard, salt, nutmeg, black pepper and hot pepper sauce; cook 15 minutes or until thickened, stirring occasionally.

3 Add broccoli; cook 15 minutes. Add carrots; cook 10 minutes or until vegetables are tender.

4 Transfer half of soup to food processor or blender; process until smooth. Return to saucepan. Add cheese product and 1 cup Cheddar; cook and stir over low heat until cheese is melted. Ladle into bowls; garnish with additional Cheddar.

GREEN CURRY WITH TOFU

MAKES 2 TO 4 SERVINGS

1 tablespoon vegetable oil

1 onion, chopped

1 package (14 ounces) firm tofu, drained and cut into 1-inch cubes

⅓ cup Thai green curry paste

1 can (about 13 ounces) coconut milk

1 broccoli crown, cut into florets

1 cup cut green beans (1-inch pieces)

½ teaspoon salt

Hot cooked brown rice or rice noodles

1 Heat oil in large skillet or wok over high heat. Add onion; cook and stir 5 minutes or until onion is soft and lightly browned.

2 Add tofu and curry paste; cook and stir 2 minutes or until curry is fragrant and tofu is coated. Add coconut milk; bring to a boil. Reduce heat to low. Add broccoli and green beans.

3 Cook 20 minutes or until vegetables are tender and sauce is thickened, stirring frequently. Taste and season with salt. Serve over rice.

BROCCOLI AND CHEESE

MAKES 4 TO 6 SERVINGS

2 medium broccoli crowns (1½ pounds), cut into florets

2 tablespoons butter

2 tablespoons all-purpose flour

1½ cups milk

½ teaspoon salt

⅛ teaspoon ground nutmeg

⅛ teaspoon ground red pepper

1 cup (4 ounces) shredded Cheddar cheese

½ cup (2 ounces) shredded Monterey Jack cheese

¼ cup shredded Parmesan cheese

Paprika (optional)

1 Bring large saucepan of water to a boil over medium-high heat. Add broccoli; cook 5 minutes or until tender.

2 Meanwhile, melt butter in medium saucepan over medium-high heat. Add flour; whisk until smooth paste forms. Gradually whisk in milk until well blended. Cook 2 minutes or until thickened, whisking frequently. Stir in salt, nutmeg and red pepper. Reduce heat to low; whisk in cheeses in three additions, whisking well after first two additions and stirring just until blended after last addition.

3 Drain broccoli; place on serving plates. Top with cheese sauce; garnish with paprika. Serve immediately.

PASTA WITH BROCCOLI PESTO

MAKES 4 SERVINGS

2 cups broccoli florets

2 cups uncooked bowtie pasta

½ cup loosely packed fresh basil leaves

5 tablespoons shredded Parmesan cheese, divided

2 tablespoons chopped walnuts, toasted*

2 tablespoons extra virgin olive oil

2 cloves garlic, crushed, divided

½ teaspoon salt

6 ounces medium cooked shrimp

¼ teaspoon black pepper

1 package (6 ounces) fresh baby spinach

1 cup halved grape tomatoes

To toast walnuts, spread in heavy skillet. Cook over medium heat 1 to 2 minutes or until nuts are lightly browned, stirring frequently.

1 Bring large saucepan of salted water to a boil. Add broccoli; cook 5 minutes or until tender. Remove to small bowl with slotted spoon; return water to a boil.

2 Add pasta to boiling water; cook according to package directions until al dente. Drain pasta; keep warm.

3 Combine broccoli, basil, 3 tablespoons cheese, walnuts, oil, 1 clove garlic and salt in food processor or blender; process until smooth. Stir into pasta in saucepan; toss to coat. Cover to keep warm.

4 Spray large skillet with nonstick cooking spray; heat over medium heat. Add shrimp, remaining 1 clove garlic and pepper; cook and stir until heated through. Stir in spinach and tomatoes; cook until spinach is wilted and tomatoes begin to soften. Add to pasta; stir gently to combine. Sprinkle with remaining 2 tablespoons cheese.

VEGGIE-PACKED SPAGHETTI AND MEATBALLS

MAKES 4 SERVINGS

8 ounces uncooked spaghetti or vermicelli

1 pound lean ground turkey or beef

1 package (10 ounces) frozen chopped spinach, thawed and pressed dry

½ cup fresh whole wheat bread crumbs*

1 egg white

1 teaspoon onion powder

1 teaspoon garlic powder

½ teaspoon black pepper

2 tablespoons olive oil

2 cups pasta sauce

2 cups (5 ounces) small broccoli florets

½ cup packaged carrots

To make fresh bread crumbs, tear 1 slice bread into pieces; process in food processor until coarse crumbs form.

1 Cook spaghetti in large saucepan of boiling salted water according to package directions to al dente. Drain and keep warm.

2 Meanwhile, combine turkey, spinach, bread crumbs, egg white, onion powder, garlic powder and pepper in medium bowl; mix well. Shape into 32 (½-inch) meatballs.

3 Heat oil in large nonstick skillet over medium heat. Add meatballs; cook 8 to 10 minutes, turning to brown all sides.

4 Add pasta sauce, broccoli and carrots to skillet. Reduce heat to medium-low; cover and simmer 8 to 10 minutes or vegetables are tender and sauce is heated through.

5 Spoon sauce and meatballs evenly over spaghetti.

BROCCOLI AND BEEF PASTA
MAKES 4 SERVINGS

1 pound ground beef

1 onion, thinly sliced

2 tablespoons tomato paste

2 cloves garlic, minced

½ teaspoon salt

½ teaspoon dried basil

½ teaspoon dried oregano

½ teaspoon dried thyme

1 can (about 14 ounces) diced tomatoes

2 cups broccoli florets

¾ cup beef broth

2 cups cooked rotini pasta

¾ cup grated or shredded Parmesan cheese, plus additional for serving

1 Cook beef and onion in large nonstick skillet over medium-high heat 6 to 8 minutes or until beef is browned and onion is tender, stirring to break up meat. Drain fat. Add tomato paste, garlic, salt, basil, oregano and thyme; cook and stir 1 minute. Add tomatoes, broccoli and broth; bring to a boil. Reduce heat to low; partially cover and simmer 20 minutes or until broccoli is tender.

2 Meanwhile, cook pasta in large saucepan of boiling salted water according to package directions for al dente. Drain and transfer to large bowl.

3 Pour sauce over pasta; add ¾ cup cheese and mix well. Sprinkle each serving with additional cheese, if desired.

BROCCOLI SLAW

MAKES 6 TO 8 SERVINGS

1 package (12 ounces) broccoli slaw

6 slices bacon, crisp-cooked and crumbled

½ small red onion, chopped

1 package (3 ounces) ramen noodles, any flavor, crumbled, divided*

¼ cup roasted salted sunflower seeds, dry roasted peanuts or slivered almonds

1 cup mayonnaise

2 tablespoons cider vinegar

1 tablespoon sugar

¼ teaspoon black pepper

Discard seasoning packet.

1 Combine broccoli slaw, bacon, onion, half of noodles and sunflower seeds in large bowl.

2 Whisk mayonnaise, vinegar, sugar and pepper in small bowl. Pour over slaw mixture; stir to combine. Garnish with remaining noodles. Serve immediately.

RICE NOODLES WITH BROCCOLI AND TOFU

MAKES 4 SERVINGS

- 1 package (14 ounces) firm or extra firm tofu
- 1 package (8 to 10 ounces) wide rice noodles
- 2 tablespoons peanut oil
- 3 medium shallots, sliced
- 6 cloves garlic, minced
- 1 jalapeño pepper, minced
- 2 teaspoons minced fresh ginger
- 3 cups broccoli florets
- ¼ cup soy sauce
- 1 to 2 tablespoons fish sauce
- Fresh basil leaves (optional)

1 Drain tofu and press between paper towels to remove excess water. Cut tofu into bite-size pieces.

2 Meanwhile, place noodles in medium bowl. Cover with hot water; let stand 15 minutes or until tender. Drain.

3 Heat oil in large skillet or wok over medium-high heat. Add tofu; stir-fry 5 minutes or until tofu is lightly browned on all sides. Transfer to bowl.

4 Add shallots, garlic, jalapeño and ginger to skillet; stir-fry 2 to 3 minutes. Add broccoli; stir-fry 1 minute. Cover and cook 3 minutes or until broccoli is crisp-tender.

5 Add tofu, noodles, soy sauce and fish sauce to skillet; stir-fry 8 minutes or until heated through. Garnish with basil.

ORECCHIETTE WITH SAUSAGE AND BROCCOLI RABE

MAKES 4 TO 6 SERVINGS

1 tablespoon olive oil

1 pound mild Italian sausage

2 cloves garlic, minced

⅛ teaspoon red pepper flakes

1½ pounds broccoli rabe, stems trimmed, cut into 2-inch pieces

1 package (16 ounces) uncooked orecchiette pasta

¾ cup grated Parmesan cheese

Salt and black pepper

1 Bring large pot of salted water to a boil. Meanwhile, heat oil in large skillet over medium-high heat. Remove sausage from casings; add to skillet. Cook sausage about 8 minutes or until browned, stirring to break up meat. Drain fat. Add garlic and red pepper flakes; cook and stir 3 minutes.

2 Add broccoli rabe to boiling water; cook 2 minutes. Remove broccoli rabe with slotted spoon; transfer to skillet with sausage mixture. Cook over medium-low heat until crisp-tender, stirring occasionally.

3 Add pasta to boiling water; cook according to package directions until al dente. Drain pasta, reserving 1 cup cooking water.

4 Combine pasta, sausage mixture and Parmesan in large serving bowl; mix well. Season with salt and pepper to taste. Stir in some of reserved cooking water if sauce is dry. Serve immediately with additional Parmesan, if desired.

SALMON AND BROCCOLI QUICHE
MAKES 4 SERVINGS

3 eggs

¼ cup chopped green onions

¼ cup plain yogurt

2 teaspoons all-purpose flour

1 teaspoon dried basil

¼ teaspoon salt

⅛ teaspoon black pepper

1 cup small broccoli florets

1 can (6 ounces) boneless skinless salmon, drained and flaked

2 tablespoons grated Parmesan cheese

1 plum tomato, thinly sliced

¼ cup fresh bread crumbs

1 Preheat oven to 375°F. Spray 1½-quart baking dish or 9-inch deep-dish pie plate with nonstick cooking spray.

2 Whisk eggs in medium bowl. Add green onions, yogurt, flour, basil, salt and pepper; whisk until well blended. Stir in broccoli, salmon and cheese. Spread evenly in prepared baking dish. Top with tomato slices and sprinkle with bread crumbs.

3 Bake 20 to 25 minutes or until knife inserted near center comes out clean. Let stand 5 minutes. Cut into wedges to serve.

CHICKEN DIVAN CASSEROLE

MAKES 6 SERVINGS

1 cup uncooked long grain rice

1 cup coarsely shredded carrots

2 tablespoons olive oil

4 boneless skinless chicken breasts

2 tablespoons butter

3 tablespoons all-purpose flour

¼ teaspoon salt

Black pepper

1 cup chicken broth

½ cup milk or half-and-half

¼ cup white wine

⅓ cup plus 2 tablespoons grated Parmesan cheese, divided

1 pound frozen broccoli florets

1 Preheat oven to 350°F. Spray 13×9-inch baking dish with nonstick cooking spray.

2 Prepare rice according to package directions. Stir in carrots. Spread mixture in prepared baking dish.

3 Heat oil in large skillet over medium-high heat. Brown chicken about 2 minutes per side. Arrange over rice.

4 For sauce, melt butter in medium saucepan over medium heat. Whisk in flour, salt and pepper; cook and stir 1 minute. Gradually whisk in broth and milk; cook and stir until mixture comes to a boil. Reduce heat; simmer 2 minutes. Stir in wine. Remove from heat. Stir in ⅓ cup Parmesan.

5 Arrange broccoli around chicken. Pour sauce over top. Sprinkle remaining 2 tablespoons Parmesan over chicken.

6 Cover and bake 30 minutes. Remove cover; bake 10 to 15 minutes or until chicken is cooked through (165°F).

WHOLE WHEAT PENNE WITH BROCCOLI AND SAUSAGE

MAKES 4 SERVINGS

8 ounces uncooked whole wheat penne pasta

1 broccoli crown, cut into florets

8 ounces mild Italian turkey sausage, casings removed

1 medium onion, quartered and sliced

2 cloves garlic, minced

2 teaspoons grated lemon peel

¼ teaspoon salt

⅛ teaspoon black pepper

⅓ cup grated Parmesan cheese

1 Cook pasta in large saucepan of boiling salted water according to package directions for al dente, adding broccoli during last 5 to 6 minutes of cooking time. Drain, place in large bowl and keep warm.

2 Meanwhile, heat large nonstick skillet over medium heat. Crumble sausage into skillet. Add onion; cook until sausage is brown, stirring to break up meat. Drain fat. Add garlic; cook and stir 1 minute.

3 Add sausage mixture, lemon peel, salt and pepper to pasta mixture; toss until blended. Sprinkle Parmesan evenly over each serving.

MACARONI AND CHEESE WITH BROCCOLI

MAKES 8 SERVINGS

2 cups (8 ounces) uncooked elbow macaroni

3 cups small broccoli florets

1 tablespoon butter

1 tablespoon all-purpose flour

½ teaspoon salt

⅛ teaspoon black pepper

1¾ cups milk

1½ cups (6 ounces) shredded sharp Cheddar cheese

1 Cook pasta in large saucepan of boiling salted water according to package directions until al dente. Add broccoli during last 5 minutes of cooking time. Drain and return to saucepan.

2 Meanwhile, melt butter in small saucepan over medium heat. Whisk in flour, salt and pepper until smooth paste form. Gradually whisk in milk in thin steady stream. Bring to a boil over medium-high heat, whisking frequently. Reduce heat and simmer 2 minutes. Remove from heat. Gradually stir in cheese until melted.

3 Add sauce to pasta and broccoli; stir until blended.

METRIC CONVERSION CHART

VOLUME MEASUREMENTS (dry)

$\frac{1}{8}$ teaspoon = 0.5 mL
$\frac{1}{4}$ teaspoon = 1 mL
$\frac{1}{2}$ teaspoon = 2 mL
$\frac{3}{4}$ teaspoon = 4 mL
1 teaspoon = 5 mL
1 tablespoon = 15 mL
2 tablespoons = 30 mL
$\frac{1}{4}$ cup = 60 mL
$\frac{1}{3}$ cup = 75 mL
$\frac{1}{2}$ cup = 125 mL
$\frac{2}{3}$ cup = 150 mL
$\frac{3}{4}$ cup = 175 mL
1 cup = 250 mL
2 cups = 1 pint = 500 mL
3 cups = 750 mL
4 cups = 1 quart = 1 L

VOLUME MEASUREMENTS (fluid)

1 fluid ounce (2 tablespoons) = 30 mL
4 fluid ounces ($\frac{1}{2}$ cup) = 125 mL
8 fluid ounces (1 cup) = 250 mL
12 fluid ounces ($1\frac{1}{2}$ cups) = 375 mL
16 fluid ounces (2 cups) = 500 mL

WEIGHTS (mass)

$\frac{1}{2}$ ounce = 15 g
1 ounce = 30 g
3 ounces = 90 g
4 ounces = 120 g
8 ounces = 225 g
10 ounces = 285 g
12 ounces = 360 g
16 ounces = 1 pound = 450 g

DIMENSIONS

$\frac{1}{16}$ inch = 2 mm
$\frac{1}{8}$ inch = 3 mm
$\frac{1}{4}$ inch = 6 mm
$\frac{1}{2}$ inch = 1.5 cm
$\frac{3}{4}$ inch = 2 cm
1 inch = 2.5 cm

OVEN TEMPERATURES

250°F = 120°C
275°F = 140°C
300°F = 150°C
325°F = 160°C
350°F = 180°C
375°F = 190°C
400°F = 200°C
425°F = 220°C
450°F = 230°C

BAKING PAN SIZES

Utensil	Size in Inches/Quarts	Metric Volume	Size in Centimeters
Baking or Cake Pan (square or rectangular)	8×8×2	2 L	20×20×5
	9×9×2	2.5 L	23×23×5
	12×8×2	3 L	30×20×5
	13×9×2	3.5 L	33×23×5
Loaf Pan	8×4×3	1.5 L	20×10×7
	9×5×3	2 L	23×13×7
Round Layer Cake Pan	8×1½	1.2 L	20×4
	9×1½	1.5 L	23×4
Pie Plate	8×1¼	750 mL	20×3
	9×1¼	1 L	23×3
Baking Dish or Casserole	1 quart	1 L	—
	1½ quart	1.5 L	—
	2 quart	2 L	—